HEART &
HUSTLE

PATRICIA BRIGHT

HEART &
HUSTLE

PATRICIA BRIGHT

ONE PLACE. MANY STORIES

HQ
An imprint of HarperCollins*Publishers* Ltd
1 London Bridge Street
London SE1 9GF

This hardback edition 2019

1

First published in Great Britain by
HQ, an imprint of HarperCollins*Publishers* Ltd 2019

A catalogue record for this book is
available from the British Library.

ISBN: 978-0-00-826310-2

Text design by Rosamund Saunders
Typeset by Palimpsest Book Production Ltd, Falkirk, Stirlingshire
Printed and bound in Great Britain by CPI Group (UK) Ltd, Croydon CR0 4YY

Dedicated to my daughter, Grace

CONTENTS

Introduction | Killing it?

I've never been someone who sits back and takes it all in. I'm not going to lie – the truth is that I often feel I'm an imposter, wondering how I got here and struggling with the idea that I might actually be any good at anything!

Take a recent fortnight: I was shot for the cover of *Glamour* magazine, nominated for a Shorty Award (think: the Oscars of social media), announced a lipstick collaboration with MAC Cosmetics and reached 2 million subscribers on my YouTube channel (which, as I'll explain, I started as a hobby to kill my boredom at uni). The week before that, I was sitting with a private equity firm discussing negotiations for a future project and organising a trip to Disneyland for my two year old. That was a busy one! But, when I'm in the moment, I don't give much thought to the immensity of what's happening. I'm on autopilot. It might look like I'm holding it all together, but I'm often scared, nervous and feel like I'm winging it as I go.

That's the reality of my life, just as it's other people's reality too. Of course I'm excited every time something great happens, but in the same moment, I'm filled with fear because it's almost too good. Still, I'm learning to appreciate every experience and achievement, and I don't take it for granted. As much as I talk about being scared, I don't let the fear stop me. It's part of the hustle and, ultimately, it drives me forward.

That's just one of the reasons why I wanted to write this book: to pull back the curtain on my experiences as a business owner and digital-content creator sharing my heart with my followers (not to mention a husband and a baby), and pass on some of the insights I've gathered along the way. In this book, I'm going to show you how to hustle like I do, using your head *and* heart. All it takes is three steps:

> Your Brand: how you can leverage who you are to kill it online and boost your work and personal life, whether you have 20 Twitter followers or 20,000.

> Your Business: how to run your side hustle like a total boss, know when to go it alone and turn your side-hustle into your full-time game.

> Your Beliefs: how to adopt certain ideas about yourself and the world that will serve you well, and ditch the thinking that's holding you back.

But before all of that, I want to reveal more about myself, to show you what I'm all about and the principles I live my life by. I've never shared the full story of why being able to look after those close to me, achieving what I set my mind to and 'securing the bag' has always been – and still is – so very important to me. So here goes …

My story: the upbringing that shaped me

I grew up in Battersea, London. I'm a south London girl for life, with African heart! My mum was a jack-of-all-trades, who loved makeup and fashion. Before she ever clapped eyes on my dad, she used to travel back and forth between London and Nigeria, where she had a salon/boutique, buying beauty and hair products to sell back home. Then, one day, she met my dad, who was also over from Nigeria, as an international student working for his university degree in the UK. It was a Clapham Junction love story – well, that's what they told me. Their eyes met across the shopping centre there, at a time when there weren't many people who looked like them in that part of south London. When they got talking, they realised they were from the same area of Nigeria, and spoke the same dialect … I suppose it was meant to be!

Not long after that, my mum became pregnant (with me), then, eighteen months later, my younger sister decided to join the party. My dad graduated with his printing technology degree and began working at a boutique publishing firm. Mum got whatever work she could, while raising two small children. But they made it work, and I have happy memories of those early days.

Then, when I was six years old, my dad was deported.

It came as a total shock. One night there was a frantic knocking at the door and a team of policemen came through the house to find my dad, before taking him away like a thief in the night. I can still clearly picture my mum sitting on the stairs pleading to deaf ears, while my sister and I sobbed. We didn't know that it would take another six years, a court case, and much sweat and tears until our father would be back with us.

Now I'm older, I understand what happened. My dad was essentially an illegal immigrant: he had outstayed his student visa and was working, but he hadn't applied for permanent residency. It was a mistake that caused a lot of pain, but that ultimately made us all a lot more resilient, as I'll explain.

Learning to hustle

Now, with Dad gone, we were on our own. When I think back on it, my mum could have let what had happened break her, but she didn't. She's about five foot, with a huge smile and doll-like eyes, completely 'butter wouldn't melt'. But, let me tell you, she's a force to be reckoned with: the most amazing example of hustle and heart.

Back then, Mum worked as a cleaner. From offices to trains, she put in the shifts, getting up in the early hours for 5 a.m. starts on some days, and trudging home after 10 p.m. finishes on others. And, while we were at primary school, my sister and I learned to put in the shifts, too. I suspect this might be considered very illegal nowadays. However, when you don't have an option, some-times you just do what you have to. Because Dad had been deported, my sister and I had to go everywhere with our mum, as she really wanted to avoid leaving us home alone.

So, at four o' clock in the morning, with sleep in our eyes and our school uniforms already on, the two of us would often go with Mum to clean offices in London. My sister and I would vacuum, wash the dishes and wipe down the surfaces – we weren't very big, but we were strong. We would put in the work then, after we had locked up the offices, Mum would take us to school.

This, of course, was a secret, and somehow (maybe it was Mum's stern looks) we knew that that part of our lives wasn't meant to be known. We'd already had an experience with the authorities and, deep down, I think we were scared that they might take our mum away like they had our dad. So we kept quiet about this part of our lives, playing at school just like all the other children.

Over the following years, I watched my mum elevate herself. She had a secondary school education and not much else, but while she still worked as a cleaner, she also began training as a nurse. She would read and study when she could and, in between her shifts and training, rustle up meals for my sister and me. Somehow Mum knew how to make a meal using basic ingredients like corned beef and packet noodles taste gourmet. Though we never had a lot in terms of material things, we never felt we lacked. There was so much love that we always felt comfortable.

Meanwhile, we were moving from council house to council house. To be honest, these places weren't great. The three of us dealt with racists, being attacked by a neighbour's dog, and the day-to-day struggle of living in what were just downright dodgy locations. Eventually, in a huge stroke of fortune, the council housed us in a lovely two-bedroom flat with carpets, freshly painted walls and even a new bunk bed that my sister and I could share. Our neighbours were relatively normal – in fact, some of them were even nice! We felt that things were on the up in our world.

At the same time, I know it was far from easy for my mum. During that time, we'd speak to Dad every week on the phone, and we visited Nigeria twice to see him while the court case was under way to try to bring him back. For years, this placed huge pressure on Mum, who just wanted to have her husband home.

Since she was now working as a nurse, doing all the shifts she could, my sister and I were often at home alone. There were a few things we always knew we mustn't do – instructions drilled into us to keep us safe. Above all, we knew not to open the door or the curtains.

And yet, Mum turned it around. Because while she was busy working all those hours, she was also saving. Eventually, she got together enough money to be able to buy the flat we were now living in off the council for £17,000 (this was in 1997). I remember the number clearly: she was rightly proud and let my sister and me know. We felt like millionaires, to own our home. Years later, after the property market went crazy, she was able to sell that flat for £250,000! Off the back of that, she bought our next home and decided to learn how to invest in property. It wasn't long before she had created her own property portfolio. With more than ten properties under her belt in seven years, she was able to become self-employed and set herself and her family up for the future. She had grinded – that's the only word for it! – her way to success.

I was in secondary school by the time Dad returned. I don't know why it took so long, but I remember being at court when the authorities finally ruled on his case. The judge said, 'I can't see why this man is not allowed to be with his wife and two children.' The upshot was that he was given permission to come back, permanently. Finally, we had our dad home. It had been a long journey. But despite that setback, my dad had continued to develop himself while he was out of the country. After getting his printing degree, he had even published some non-fiction books. On his return to the UK, things had changed significantly in that world, so he went on to study law and work within the immigration services – the irony! (I draw qualities from both parents: my dad's more academic, whereas my mum's a hustler. Put it together and you get me, in the middle.)

The blueprint for my success

Despite things often being difficult, I can't regret the lessons of those tough years. Through all my childhood experiences, I had been learning something that has shaped the path of my whole life: that it's within your own power to change your situation. Mum showed me, through her example, that what you expect of yourself is usually what you will achieve. Her limitations and the circumstances of her life were mere obstacles to work around – it wasn't so much that she didn't see them, but she simply didn't focus on them.

Similarly, it might not seem like you're on the road to success – perhaps you sure as hell don't fit the traditional mould of someone who's on their way up – but who cares? A stranger watching my mum graft away on her cleaning shifts, kids in tow, would have struggled to predict where she'd end up. And this is something that, even today, motivates me throughout my journey: the truth is, whether your path to your goals looks like it's 'supposed' to look doesn't matter. As you'll learn from the stories I'm going to share, there have been many occasions where it looked like the odds were stacked against me, but I've achieved goals anyway – and you can, too.

• •

LIFE LESSON: Your past doesn't have to define your future. As my mum taught me through her hard work and hustle, things don't have to stay the same: you can change your situation. You can change your life.

• •

I also learned from Mum the power of thought and words. She was – is – always positive about herself and her situation (sometimes, it can seem, to the point of delusion!). That's why one of my favourite proverbs is, 'Life and death are in the power of the tongue … so speak life'. What that means to me is that the spoken word is incredibly powerful: you have to speak positively to yourself. And, in the same way, you have to see the good in your situation and stay hopeful. You never know what your story will be – but, regardless of your situation, if you give in to negative thoughts and put out negative words, negativity will be the result. It's not 'fate', it's the power of your brain and will: if you don't think and feel like you *can*, then you probably *won't*. That's something I've held onto over the years, and through every adversity I've faced.

We're all human

There's one more thing it's important to remember: the way things are portrayed on social media can have us all seeing things through rose-tinted glasses. In a world filled with meticulously planned feeds and carefully selected, glamorous images, it's easy to get the impression that other people are living the 'perfect life'. And those with the most interaction online, with likes and comments streaming in, must be in a great position, right? Well, what I know, and have seen and experienced first-hand, is that behind the attractive photos, upbeat videos and funny status updates, will lie a long, winding journey filled with ups and downs. Everyone has experiences that can't be corrected with a pretty filter, and that will likely not be shared with the world. That doesn't mean they didn't happen. It's normal and it's real life. Nowadays, I can look back at my hard times and know they have provided me with the head, heart and hustle (in other words, the mental attitude, the emotional resilience and the ability to grind) that have propelled me along the journey I am on today.

I'll give a few examples. At one point, I didn't have any friends. At another, I was made redundant from my job in the City. I also broke up with Mike, the man I thought was going to be my 'forever guy' (he's now my husband, so go figure!). Another time, I quit my job to be a full-time YouTuber and that didn't work out so well … as you'll find out. But all those experiences have helped to shape me as an individual and lead me to the place I am at now.

Take the situation with my friends – or lack of them. That came about when, at university, I was sharing a house with a roommate. We didn't argue, but the atmosphere grew very cold and distant quite quickly. Even today, I can't pinpoint exactly what the issue was: it was all unsaid, which was harder to resolve. I found solace in the online world. When she'd go out, I'd go straight upstairs and get on to my computer. There, I was able to escape my reality, distracting myself by getting deep into the world of makeup, hair and beauty – things I'd always loved, but had never had anyone to chat to about passionately. I started on a picture-sharing forum for women who wanted to grow their hair, improve their skin, and slay their makeup, where you could also write comments: Fotki, the Reddit of all things beauty. I would spend hours reading through people's profiles, following their journeys to a greater glow and even longer hair. They would share pictures and then eventually move on to video: that was my fix before Instagram! You could swap tips and share praise. 'Oh my gosh,' we'd tell each other, 'your hair has grown so much. And your skin looks great!'

I wouldn't let anybody in my real life know that I could spend hours on these forums. How crazy would I sound talking about my weekend with a garlic and mayo scalp mix slathered on my hair, an egg face mask on and sweet potato skins on my eyes? It wasn't really bragging material. Some people would mix hair-growth stimulants and sulphur with oil! (I don't recommend you try that.) Or, they'd share unusual ideas such as the inversion method – tipping your head upside down and giving yourself a scalp massage to stimulate blood flow (also a headache). But we hoped an enviable head of hair would result! We'd set ourselves challenges and update each other every day on what we were doing. Looking back, what we were into was pretty niche, but it was amazing to be part of a community of like-minded people. Some people are into computer games and films, some of us are into the finer things in life, like sulphur mixes! All the time, I was tapping away, immersing myself in this world that I loved.

Now that I look back, I think, *What the hell was I up to?* It does make me laugh. But the people on those forums really did something for me, though they didn't know it: they saved me when I didn't have any friends. (And, I do have to say, my hair was so much healthier in my days of mayo masks – really full and thick!) What's more, my time online back then led me to my career today. I was spending all this time on these forums looking at photos and watching a ton of videos on all things hair and beauty, and eventually fashion-related content too. I had fallen in love – and knew that I wanted to do *this*. What 'this' was I wasn't sure, but that didn't stop me. So, while still a student, I bought a cheap camera – you couldn't just use your phone to film in those days – and started recording.

My first YouTube video was just a minute and a half long, introducing me to the world … or so I hoped. 'Hi, I'm Patricia. This is my new channel.' I probably had an American twang, because I was watching so many people who did. 'I'm going to do fashion,' I announced. 'I'm going to do makeup. K, see you, bye.' That was pretty much it. I was staring into the lens, trying to be quite sultry! Back then, I imitated people I liked, so it wasn't very me, but that didn't matter. It was a start.

My second video was a 'haul' – which was basically like sitting down with your girlfriends and sharing with them what bargains you were able to pick up at the stores. Back then, I used to go vintage shopping and so I showed off some of the items I had bought. And my third was a DIY, where I put buttons and trims onto a few Primark tops. I remember the moment I finally reached ten views. I was so excited, until I realised it was because I had refreshed the page ten times – they were all *my* views! Still, I gradually started to get a few people checking me out. I used to comment on other people's videos, and sometimes they would comment back and watch mine. I'd think, *Oh my God, they've noticed me!* And then, I just kept going ... So, although in my real life I was quite lonely, I was connecting in the digital space – and something truly great came of it.

Always remember: you never know how your story is going to turn out. You will go through sticky moments, as I did, and still do, and you might not enjoy every step along the road, but I promise you the results will be worth it. All the good things that have happened for me didn't happen overnight, or without hard work, but they did happen, and they can for you too. YOU have control! And even when it's really tough, it's still not as hard as waking up in five years' and realising you could have started turning your life around five years ago – but you're still exactly where you were back then. So buckle up. YOU are in the driving seat!

Let's make a start – going all the way back to the beginning ...

1| Natural-born hustler

Everyone starts from somewhere – and usually it's not the place where we want to be. As Drake puts it, 'Started from the bottom'. Most of us, even if we want to build a long-term hustling strategy, start out working for someone else. That doesn't mean you won't – like me – eventually become your own boss. Although, funnily enough, I did start out as my own boss …

Growing up grinding

Even before I ever had a job, I was earning money from the age of thirteen. I knew I had to get my hustle on early, because nothing was going to be handed to me on a plate. As a kid, I didn't get pocket money – I got dinner money, and that was about it. My parents (Dad being back in the UK by this point) weren't stingy, but they wanted me to learn how to look after what I had. So, I'd be given my £10 or £15 for the week, and then I could do whatever I wanted with it. A lot of it went on McDonald's pancakes and sausage for breakfast, but I tried to be smart and save at least

£2 per week here and there, even if that meant skipping the school lunch and making my own sandwiches at home.

But there was nothing spare to have fun with. I thought that there must be a way to get around this – I didn't have to be broke. So it was only natural that I decided to use my head and figure out ways to make some cash. I'd taught myself how to do braids and cornrows, having watched my mum do my sister's hair, and had eventually become the family's resident hairstylist. For aunties and cousins, I was the go-to girl, and I loved it. I did hair like it was therapy, and practised a lot on myself. At secondary school, I was beginning to get a lot of attention because of it. Girls would say to me admiringly, 'Your hair is so nice.' I'd tell them I did it myself, and they'd ask me to do theirs. Cha-ching! I saw my opportunity and started a little business. I became the playground stylist, and for £5 half a head and £10 a full head, I would do whatever they wanted: zigzags, patterns and other designs. Soon I had regular clients and could make what my parents gave me for a week in a single day. Now I had the extra money I wanted for ice lollies and McD's pancakes – the finer things in life!

Entering the workforce

I got my first ever job when I was fourteen, delivering kitchenware catalogues and any subsequent orders to houses. Yes, I knocked door to door offering a catalogue listing all the fancy utensils you didn't know you needed! I'd do this during the school holidays, accompanied by a few other kids from the local area. I don't know how legal it all was, but we were doing it anyway! The adult accompanying us was a neighbour, a well-respected man in the area who everyone liked, with that 'Del Boy' East London charm. Mum was happy to see that we were going out and earning some coin. And so we'd be dropped off from street to street, handing out catalogues one week, delivering orders and collecting payments the next. We earned a pittance in commission from every order that customers made. Despite that, if I worked all summer I could easily make £200 by the end of it, and as a kid that honestly felt like a lot of good, hard-earned money. I was proud.

In fact, I put those summers of work experience on my CV, which helped me to get my first 'real' job, in retail. I had just turned sixteen and was at sixth form when a shopping mall opened up nearby in Croydon. It was new and shiny with a super posh department store called House of Fraser. I remember writing up my CV, listing out my skills and of course jazzing up my work experience. All that knocking on doors had to count for something! It had helped me to develop my 'customer service' skills, I wrote. Packing up orders honed my 'organisational skills', while taking door-to-door cash payments was my 'financial management' experience. And just like that, I had myself a job. I'd leave school on a Thursday in my work uniform – occasion wear by Coast, the store I worked at in House of Fraser – so I'd be on the bus in my shiny satin skirt. It really was a look! My working hours were 6 p.m. till 10 p.m. every Thursday, all day Saturday, and occasionally a Sunday.

For the next four years, including part of my time at university, that was my routine. In all honesty, sometimes I hated it. Late-night Thursdays could drag, while in retail the customers are always right (even when they're not! That's just how it goes). Being on fitting-room duty wasn't exactly stimulating, and I often found myself clock-watching. But despite not enjoying it much, it was my hustle at the time, and the company looked after me when I went to university in Manchester. There, I was transferred to Selfridges and when I needed to move again, they transferred me into their new sister store, Oasis. In all, I worked within that company for almost four years. It paid for a whole lot, and kept me busy and potentially out of trouble.

While I was at university in Manchester, I also went back to my secondary-school side hustle. Rather than the playground, my halls of residence and student accommodation were now my shop floor. By that point, I'd taught myself how to do weaves, extensions and even chemical relaxers. I wasn't a trained salon professional (and I would never advise doing this; people should go to salons to have chemical treatments), but at-home relaxer kits were available and, growing up, I'd never gone to a professional salon to have my treatments. At university there were plenty of students who wanted their hair done, and I took full advantage of this. I had a set rate, the proper kit, and soon a new list of regular clients, some of who would even travel from other cities to see me. For every relaxer, weave or braids I did, I was earning £30, £40, £50 a time, matching what I could make at my part-time job in retail. Growing up, I'd had no idea that not having the money to go to the salon would turn out to be an advantage, forcing me to learn skills that would later help me earn money.

My first business failure

Mind you, my ventures didn't always work out, because that's the reality of life and business. Another side hustle I set up was a beauty community. I wanted to bring girls together who loved makeup but couldn't afford the typical retail prices. I'd found a distributor online that sold MAC makeup and other well-known brands, and I honestly couldn't believe the prices. While store prices were anywhere between £12 and £15 per eye shadow or lipstick, this guy had these same products on sale for £3. By anyone's calculation it was a bargain. Even if I sold them for £9 each, I was going to make a profit, right?

So I spent my money on stock, investing a few hundred pounds, which was a lot for me at the time. I printed out flyers and organised a space at the student union for my event. Then, my stock came in. It looked great from afar, but on closer inspection all was not as it seemed. For a start, the spelling on the packaging was wrong: 'MAC' was spelt 'NAC'. That wasn't all. The labels on the backs of the items didn't look like the labels on the products you could buy in store, and the colours were all off. I realised I had been ripped off. The products were trash and very, very fake. I learned that day, if something seems too good to be true, it probably is. I'd got burned, but I was also growing. Slowly but surely I was developing my skills as a 'multi-hustler' – someone with multiple sources of income.

Real-world expectations

I'd already been working, in one way or another, for years when I finished university. But that didn't mean I was relaxed about the future. I want to take a moment to talk about my university experience – what I was doing when I wasn't busy with all my jobs and side hustles! So let's rewind for a second.

When I was at school, it had always been expected that I'd go to university, and, grades-wise, I did OK. In sixth form I studied biology, chemistry, psychology, business studies – all academic subjects, but when it came to applying any of these to real life, I didn't want to. I wanted to study fashion! After all, it was my passion, right? I found a fashion and marketing university course, which got me super-excited. Initially my parents were a bit unsure about it: 'Fashion? You don't want to be a doctor or a lawyer?' But I wasn't deterred. It was full steam ahead (well, for a season at least!).

But early on in that course, I realised it wasn't for me. I was hating it! My passion was fashion, but not in that context. I didn't connect with the people on my course and, more importantly, I didn't warm to the subject matter in the university setting. My expectations simply didn't match reality. In one class, a group of us designed a single shirt with four seams. I thought, *What the hell is this?* I didn't want to make clothes or cut out patterns. At the same time, I found out the graduate salary in the fashion industry at the time was around £10,000 to £12,000 a year – for a starter role at a huge sports brand, for example. I thought, *Hold on, can that really be the salary after all these years, not to mention the cost, of university?* Hell, no! I had a reality check: it was hard to understand how the salary could be that low, considering the effort and commitment I was going to put in. I remember thinking, *This is not enough, especially for what I want to achieve for my future.* I couldn't risk continuing as a fashion student when I wasn't sure if it would support me or my future family. I needed more security.

Some people are fortunate enough to have parents fund them when they're getting started. I didn't have that option. I wasn't resentful, but I knew that I was going to regret it if I didn't make a more financially stable choice for my future. In hindsight, my past-life experiences likely contributed to my craving for security. As it happened, one part of the fashion course I did enjoy and found fairly easy was the accounting module. The cogs were turning … I said to myself, *You know what? I'm going to do accounting and finance.*

The way I see it, life goes in seasons. I figured that if I stuck with the fashion course, it wasn't going to set me up in the way that I wanted. So I switched, believing that afterwards I'd be able to get a better job, earn more money, and that would provide me with more freedom and opportunities. I wasn't necessarily going to be an accountant all my life – and, I was right, that's not what happened – but I wanted to give myself options. I didn't necessarily love my new course, but I realised my mind really connected with the subject matter. I liked the spreadsheets and crunching numbers – I'm analytical. Changing my path was right for me.

I learned an important lesson through that. When you're starting off, it's important to find that sweet spot between your passion, your ability and what's practical. You don't have to start off in your dream job or career – most of us have got to pay the bills somehow, right? In the US, young workers now switch jobs on average four times in their first ten years after graduation.[1] My approach is to think big, and take small steps.

---

1 According to a study by LinkedIn: www.ft.com/content/0151d2fe-868a-11e7-8bb1-5ba57d47eff7

• •

LIFE LESSON: When it comes to life, it's never a straight line — it's more like a zigzag! Think of every experience, good and bad, as a stepping stone to the next opportunity.

• •

But Patricia, what should *I* do?

The short and honest answer is: I don't know, the answer is different for everybody! But I will tell you something: where you start off doesn't matter as much as you think. For example, the thing about studying is that it's not just about the subject you choose. The skills that you pick up and the people you meet along the way can be even more valuable. Some degrees, like medicine and dentistry, are vocational, of course, but otherwise much of the experience is about learning the skills to equip you for life in general, rather than for a particular job. Things like understanding how to think critically, analyse, research independently, and even just how to be someone who can show up, sit down and meet deadlines on time. Of course, not everybody wants to carry on studying after school, and often for those people university can be an expensive waste of three years! The days where having any degree was considered highly prestigious and a guaranteed ticket to a life of comfort and good income are long gone.

The problem is, when you're younger, you don't really know what career options are out there. It all seems very rigid – lawyer, accountant, doctor, nurse – but there are so many more options that you have no idea about, and what's available changes as the world changes. You can even write your own job role aligned to your strengths, bring it to a company and say, 'I will do this for you', and they might agree – and pay you a salary to do that!

No wrong jobs

In the same way, we have a tendency to get really connected to our first job, thinking it's a lot more important than it actually is; we believe that we'll be 'stuck there for life' and it's nothing like the area we want to work in. Sometimes you'll hear people say, 'There's certain things I wouldn't do,' or 'I can't do that, I've got a degree!' But pretty much any job is better than sitting around holding out for the perfect starter role.

As I've tried to show you by explaining my own first jobs and hustles, I've come to learn that all experience is valuable and can be a springboard to greater things in the future. Working in a kitchen, for example, will teach you time management, teamwork and how to cope under pressure. Data entry will teach you how to stay focused and, at a basic level, to turn up and get the work done even when it bores you! You just have to remember that if you're doing something you don't like, you don't have to do it for ever – but you may have to do it for now. I've had people work for me who studied at Oxford University alongside those who have left school at eighteen and worked jobs some would consider 'menial'. But what I've learned is that ultimately it doesn't matter whether someone's got a degree or not. It's all about whether someone can apply themselves to a task, even if it isn't the most glamorous thing to do, and deliver results. Success lies in the ability to learn and consistently execute.

· ·

LIFE LESSON: Sometimes you have to do the lower-paying job or the role you're not so keen on, to build up the experience that will put you where you want to be.

· ·

So by all means have a plan – but keep your options open. You don't want to close yourself off to opportunity. You never know where your next break might come from. In my own case, after university, I ended up in the City, in the high-flying world of big investment banks. It wasn't an industry I knew or where I had family that could get me an 'in', and I really didn't have a clue how it all worked. So how did I do it? Let me explain …

Use your network

I've always had that overriding sense that I'll be fine, a mentality I picked up from my mum. I felt somehow I'd be successful, but how – or even what my definition of success was – I really didn't know. But, as I neared the end of my university course, I did have a wonderful friend from college, Emeka, who was doing a computer science degree at Manchester University. He was a bright guy, going places, and I would confide in him because he inspired me and his door was always open. I would ask him a ton of questions about everything – love, life, careers. Nearing the end of our courses, I happened to ask him what he was doing after uni and whether he'd heard about any opportunities. I was worried. I had no idea what I was going to do next. He shared with me that his friend had just got offered work at an investment bank called Merrill Lynch and was getting paid £30,000 for his first job. Emeka himself was about to do a summer internship there. I was shocked: that seemed a lot of money and a great opportunity. I wanted in. Emeka encouraged me to apply for an internship. He gave me the recruiter's email, I got in touch with her and she told me there was a Women in Technology dinner taking place, aimed at female students interested in going into the City. Women who had senior roles in technology at Merrill Lynch – directors and heads of departments – would be attending. I wasn't a tech girl and I knew nothing about the City, so I got my friend to give me the lowdown. In fact, I prepared for this 'networking dinner' like it was an exam (although it was super-casual). When the evening arrived, I was ready with my note pad, pen and article clippings to stand out.

The night of the dinner, I quickly noticed the other students were chit-chatting among themselves and not talking to the women who had come from the business. I'm not sure if nerves or hunger were to blame, but I decided to take it upon myself to work the room, dropping in references to all the research I'd done. When it came to the sit-down part of the evening, I was that annoying person with my hand up to ask questions related to the industry: 'What's it like being a woman in the business?', 'Where do you see the financial markets going?' The women from the bank seemed slightly taken aback, to be honest – *Why is she asking these questions?* – but they were intrigued. And I wanted to stand out: I was hustling. That didn't mean I wasn't perfectly nice to everyone there. You can be nice – and totally shameless! But I was focused on what I wanted from that encounter, whereas the others were a bit more laid back about connecting with the executives from the bank. I'd gone prepared, and the executives remembered me.

Preparation is key in a situation where you want to impress. You don't have to think of clever questions off the cuff. If you're shy or unsure, put together a mental 'cheat sheet' for the conversation ahead. In my case, I'd spoken to my friend Emeka, picking his brains about what I could ask, and I knew what subjects I hoped to talk about.

While I was never going to be exactly like my friend, I *could* learn from him. He even read my statements for my internship application – 'you could put this in', 'watch out, that looks wrong' – and mentioned 'my friend Patricia' to the recruiters, so they looked out for me. Some people suggest seeking out mentors, even people you might respect that you've never met before. Go for it if it feels right for you, but you don't have to do it that way. My friend was my mentor – even if he didn't know that (till now!).

• •

LIFE LESSON: Associate with people who are doing what you want to do, but who are doing it better than you. Don't be threatened – you can climb together. I knew my friend was more informed than me, I knew he was on a really good trajectory, so my attitude was: *Mate – hook me up!* And that's exactly what he did.

• •

Acing the interview

Soon I learned that I'd passed the first hurdle: I'd been selected for the interview process. But how do you get that great job or secure that fantastic internship when you've no experience? It's the classic frustrating catch-22 situation for a lot of graduates, school-leavers and career-switchers. Again, it's all about preparation and accumulating a working knowledge of the industry you want to enter. But, at the same time, when you're starting off no one's expecting you to be an absolute expert in, say, financial markets. You'll learn everything when you're on the job. The key thing is just to demonstrate what skill sets you have. Now, when I was chasing this Merrill Lynch internship, I hadn't done a placement in the City already and therefore couldn't draw on experiences I hadn't had. So I talked about what I did know: I'd always worked in retail, and I had my hair business. I wove narratives – told compelling stories about my experiences – to show the recruiters that I had experience in something.

In my case, I had what seemed like endless interviews. There was a woman quite close to me in age who was in HR – the gatekeeper. Then, there were a panel of men in suits. But my approach was the same: charm, share, talk! You don't have to be embarrassed about your past experience – draw on it to show, for example, how you dealt with difficult situations or how you took the initiative. So much of work and business is firefighting: share how you put out flames, what you learned, and showcase your ability to come up with solutions. This is exactly what I look for today in my team members: that story about the tricky customer you managed to deliver for really can serve you well.

I'd also done lots of unpaid activities that packed my CV. I'd been a mentor to school-age kids and shared with them what it was like being a university student. And I was involved with Young Enterprise, a scheme helping young people set up their own businesses. I was able to draw from both experiences. So get involved in real-life activities! If you're at home twiddling your thumbs or always staring at a screen you'll have nothing to draw from. Your experiences can help you get that role, though they might seem unrelated to the job. Sometimes recruiters simply want to know that you're a well-rounded person.

• •

LIFE LESSON: Business is about people working with people. You want to connect with the interviewer. Preparation is important of course, but once you're in there don't be afraid to let go of the pressure to remember every tiny detail. You don't need to remember to ask what happened to the company's tech division in the last quarter. Try to be a little more personal and find common ground.

• •

Break the rules

I know a lot of people can feel scared about applying for jobs. The list of requirements can seem so daunting! And this lack of confidence in our abilities seems to affect women in particular. You might have heard this statistic before: men will apply for a job when they meet just 60 per cent of the requirements, but women only apply if they meet 100 per cent of them.[1] It's been called the 'gender confidence gap' – we can be hesitant about taking action to push ourselves forward.

My thinking is: just do it – even if you're not sure of the outcome, try it and see what happens. When I applied for the internship, the odds were stacked against me. I knew I didn't have the grades they wanted. I wasn't in my second year of university, like most applicants, but in my final year. The bank required 360 UCAS points to apply, but because I had dropped an A-level (chemistry – I hated it!) I only had 280 points. That, in normal circumstances, would have automatically taken me out of the running for most of the graduate schemes I was interested in. But I completed the application form, despite my situation. Some people would have thought to themselves, 'I don't have the right grades so I'm not going to apply' – to be honest, that's what I thought at first! I had never submitted any other similar applications because I was scared of rejection. But, encouraged by my friend Emeka, I did it despite my fear, explaining honestly why I didn't have the UCAS points, and why it wasn't an issue. In that way, I set the ball rolling for my future.

Later, as part of that process to get an internship, I failed one of the maths tests. I cried straight after taking it, as I knew it hadn't gone well. With thousands of people applying for the internship programme, I knew that if you failed one of the tests,

1 From a Hewlett Packard internal report: https://hbr.org/2014/08/why-women-dont-apply-for-jobs-unless-theyre-100-qualified

you didn't get in – that was the general rule. But because I had tried to build those relationships at the dinner, and connected with a few of the right people – because they'd seen my drive and determination first-hand and considered my potential to be more important than my ability – they gave me the opportunity to come in and retake the test. This time I made sure I was ready. The questions were mainly algebra (my nemesis!), so I spent a few weeks improving my knowledge of the principles, doing practice test after practice test, night after night. When it was time to do the real test again, I smashed it and got the internship.

• •

LIFE LESSON: Your limits are based on how you perceive yourself. Challenge your perception and you might be surprised. Every time I hit a stumbling block, I might have been momentarily disheartened, but I pushed through and the results were better than I could ever have imagined. Sometimes that's all you have to do: push through.

• •

The upshot was, I graduated, did my three-month internship in London, then was offered a job at the bank! I couldn't believe it. My starting salary was £35,000, with a £5,000 sign-on bonus. For a twenty-one-year-old, that's a lot of money. I'd done it! I thought to myself, *I'm rich! I've made it in life.*

Of course, I didn't know then but this was just the beginning. And we'll get into my time as a full-time employee. But I want to stress that as much as I talk about 'doing your own thing' and being an entrepreneur, I 100 per cent appreciate the values I picked up in the workplace. The skills I gained from all of my collective experiences and side hustles brought me to where I am today, providing me with valuable knowledge and experience that university could never have given me.

Nail that interview

It can be difficult to get that crucial first role and the dreaded interview can be a major stumbling block. But a good interview can also be the most impactful thing you do. So I'm going to share my cheats to make it a little less painful:

> You do not have to know everything – what you want to show is that you are willing to learn everything.

> Draw on your experiences to give specific examples of what you would do in the role. For example, '*If scenario X happened I would do Y, because when I dealt with situation A I applied B and XYZ was the result.*'

> There are a lot of cookie-cutter questions (some of which I've listed below) you can be asked, so prep a response for each one that has a little more fire than, 'I've always wanted to work for this company because [insert what you read on their online bio].'

> Practise your interview technique out loud. Yes, it could be embarrassing but it makes a difference. Find a friend to ask you questions and practise your response. Alternatively, you can find a mirror and practise with yourself.

> INHALE. EXHALE. SMILE!

The old chestnuts

Think of strong responses to the following before you walk into the interview room (and keep them safe for future use):

> Why do you want this job/internship?

> Why should I hire you?

> What can you bring to the role or the organisation?

> What relevant experience do you have?

> What relevant skills to you have?

> Where do you see yourself in five years'? (Progressing within that company, of course!)

> What are your strengths?

> What are your weaknesses? (Talk about areas in which you're already improving and what strategy you're applying to do this. You want to be honest but not *too* honest.)

> And if you're thrown a curveball? Don't panic. Take a moment to think, then take a stab at the most sensible, thoughtful answer you can reach for. So much of this is about delivery. Be enthusiastic, respectful, and make eye contact – you'll have them eating out of your hand in no time!

2 | Yes, I work for myself on the internet!

I do sometimes get tired of answering the *'What* is it you do?' question I hear time and time again, coupled with the 'Is that even a job?' remark IRL. But in the digital space, people like me get a different reaction. I see a lot of #GIRLBOSS, #HUSTLE and #Buildingmyempire hashtags, sprinkled with copious amounts of praise in the comments. It can make it look like going it alone is the most exciting thing in the world – the one thing everyone should be aiming for. In 2017, it's estimated that nearly 660,000 companies were started in the UK, a new record – and that figure is expected to be broken year-on-year.[1] So what's the truth?

The myths around being your own boss ...

WARNING: I'm going to bust some myths around being in the coveted role of boss. 'Entrepreneur' has become a bit of a buzzword of late, and it can feel like being an employee is second

---

1 According to the Centre for Entrepreneurs, a UK think tank: https://www.ft.com/content/cb56d86c-88d6-11e7-afd2-74b8ecd34d3b

best. But some people are amazing employees, great at hustling within their roles and climbing the ladder. They love the structure, they like the industry they're in and they're able to deliver consistently. My sister, my dad and my husband are all amazing employees. Never missing a day of work, they thrive. And being an employee can offer a great work-life balance and lots of stability, depending on the job you do. I've worked with some amazing 'employees' – my bosses and other senior executives around me – who were making a huge impact in their industries and the wider world. There is plenty of power and skill involved in being a mover and shaker in the workforce. Doctors, nurses and members of the armed forces for example, are all employees, providing essential services.

Meanwhile, some people think being self-employed means a life where you can wake up when you want, go to bed when you want, go out when you want, in between drinking champagne on a yacht. Well, that ain't it! While being self-employed, I've learned that it involves sacrifices bigger than I could have ever imagined, that income is not guaranteed, that you can lose all you achieved in a second, and that you can end up working round the clock. I may have to have a call with partners in China at 1 a.m., or a call with clients in LA at 9 p.m. – 'free time' is not in my vocabulary.

Of course I'm grateful for everything I've achieved. I've had so many amazing experiences. But I don't mind saying that there are times when I wish I could just go back to one of my regular jobs. Even though I'm established, I work ten times harder than I used to as an employee (at least, it feels that way!) because there's a little voice in my head telling me that it won't last for ever. I've got to always be thinking ten steps ahead: *if everything crumbles, what would I do?* With that in mind, I've made sure I have some money saved up and a back-up plan, just in case I ever need to make the switch to something else. If it all disappears, I'll go into marketing and digital advertising, because it's what I know about and genuinely enjoy. In fact, that would be my dream career if I wasn't doing what I'm doing. That's my plan B and I think everyone should have one. Having a back-up plan doesn't for a second mean I'm not pushing full steam ahead and committed to the path I'm on, but it gives me peace of mind.

... And about being an influencer

So now we've covered 'girlboss' myths, let's move on to those around being a social media influencer – and if you've picked up this book it's probably something you want to know more about. I know there are lots of misconceptions. The thing I hear most often is that we make money for doing nothing. The reality is that we're just like most self-employed people. We are creating, distributing, working with customers and partners, we're investing thousands of pounds in our equipment and we're at risk of losing all of it at the drop of a hat. Like everyone who works for themselves, we have sleepless nights and worry about what's going to happen next. For those who want job security, who want consistency, who want guaranteed money, who want overnight success, this isn't the industry. You can be popular today, and – one Twitterstorm later – public enemy number one. You can find yourself working for free for weeks for the 'exposure' (which you can't pay a mortgage with). You can even work for an agreed fee for months and not receive a penny. There is no trade union for bloggers!

HOW I LOST £60K

Cue my own horror story. In the not too distant past, I worked on a number of projects with huge brands via an agency. These were very recognisable brands and, when I was approached to create content for them, I was beyond excited to have been considered for the work. The payment terms were three months, which was a long time to wait to be paid, but I was willing to take the risk bearing in mind their calibre. I delivered video content for the brands and it was shared globally on their social platforms. My face was everywhere, and I was really proud.

But three days before my payment was due, I received a call that the agency involved in the deal had gone bankrupt ... and I had lost £60,000 in one fell swoop. At the time, I had a three-month-old baby, a mortgage and a loft conversion that still needed to be paid for. Yep, that happened. In a moment of delirium I actually laughed, and then I cried. I spoke to my solicitors and my accountant. 'Unfortunately, the agency have to pay all their creditors first, and maybe in five years from now, you might get a pittance after they've paid their landlords, their taxes and their employees, who haven't been paid their salaries.' I was at the back of the queue. I then reached out to the brands that still had my content on their platforms, and asked if there was anything they could do. I received one uniform response: no.

A number of other influencers were in the same situation, so I wasn't alone. I'm not holding my breath for that money now. And, of course, stories like this aren't confined to the social media world. Talking to other people who run their own businesses, I've learned that it's all part of the wild ride. I tell you all this to show you that the life of an influencer is not all filters and flights.

Now the good news

Haven't put you off yet? Good! Because, despite all the risks, I absolutely love working for myself and running my own business, especially one based around social media. It's true – being an entrepreneur is not easy and it's not for everyone. But for those who do want to be their own boss and are willing to put in the work, it's incredibly rewarding. The career I've built means I get to go to wonderful places; I get to try new products and test everything out before it hits the market; and I get to create my own product-based businesses, all because of the relationship I have with my online community. And most importantly, I get to share what I enjoy every single day with people who actually want to hear it. That's crazy!

Those are the highlights for me. For others it may be the autonomy they enjoy, or the flexibility in terms of organising their life outside of a traditional office. In fact, there's research showing that, despite not knowing where the next pay cheque is coming from, self-employed people are happier than employees. A recent study from the universities of Sheffield and Exeter involving 5,000 people from around the world found that those who worked for themselves 'were not only amongst the most engaged but also experienced greater opportunities for innovation, achieving challenging targets and meeting high standards'.[1] All that, plus you get to dodge the rush-hour commute #WINNING. Even if you don't want to go it alone – or not yet, anyway – lots of what I'm going to tell you still applies. Because, really, you're always working for yourself and your future (whatever your manager thinks).

---

1 https://www.theladders.com/career-advice/these-are-the-happiest-people-at-work

How I started (stumbled into) being an 'entrepreneur'

So, as you already know, I got my start in the City. I had a good salary, but meanwhile I continued my hobby of posting YouTube videos on the side. In time, I started making a small amount of money from the adverts played alongside my videos here and there, which was a nice bonus. I remember when I received my first payment from Google AdSense (I'd signed up to their programme that puts advertising on your content) of £60! When I saw it on the computer screen, I was so happy that I could make a little extra cash for drinks and so on, simply by doing something I enjoyed in my free time. I'd only been going for a year or two, making videos on fashion, beauty and makeup, and at this point I still didn't expect this to be my main business. If anything, I was spending way more on clothing, makeup and camera equipment than I was making, as I enjoyed it so much! I remember one of my early requests, as a present from my hubby, was for a new camera costing around £200, which felt like a lot at the time. Back then, my friends and family were surprised that I was spending so much on something that was, after all, just a hobby. Little did they know that I was investing in my future.

After a while that £60 turned into £600. But I was totally naive, and didn't know to tell the taxman about it. I was just enjoying the additional income. I found out later that not declaring this extra income would come back to bite me in the butt … but for now I was blissfully unaware. My career continued to move forward, and despite being made redundant from my first job during huge staff cuts, I was able to move on to working as a consultant in the City, then within an international financial institution.

But, even though I was becoming more and more settled in my career, the hobby that I'd been busy with in the evenings and every weekend for the past few years had begun to make me £2,000–£3,000 every month, and I was starting to receive offers for work and collaborations from companies and brands. Almost without meaning to, I'd developed my hobby into a fully fledged side business that was close to matching my City salary!

My first big deal

I remember when I booked my first four-figure deal with a brand. I didn't have a specific fee or rate, and there was no rulebook or precedent that I knew of in terms of making money online. I'd been used to charging a few hundred pounds here and there to partner with brands, which I was happy with (considering that I'd been making all my content for free prior to that). Then one day I was approached by a production company who wanted me to make some videos for a fairly big brand. I remember the lady from the company saying in an email that they only had '3' for the work, which I took to mean three hundred pounds. While I would have accepted that, the hustler in me said I wanted '4'. She responded to say that she couldn't manage '4' but that she could offer £3,500! The whole time she'd meant £3,000! By accident I had stumbled into finding out that I could potentially make enough out of this hobby to turn it into a business. That deal, coupled with my Google AdSense income, meant that was the first month I actually earned more than my monthly salary. My revenue was growing!

That experience was a real eye-opener. When I got married to Mike, what I generated through my channel contributed to the budget for our wedding, and went towards the deposit on our first house. But I wasn't getting too carried away. I wasn't prepared to leave the prestige of my City job, or the potential to be a senior manager or even partner, for a quick buck. I decided that I would keep up my hobby posting videos online on the side, while also maintaining the steady income and security from my day job ... I was 'multi-hustling'.

And I was learning so much along the way. As more work came in, I began to standardise my process by auto-responding to emails, creating a rate card, and putting aside set times to manage the business side of my social media profile. Before long, I was booking three to four projects a month, and making double to triple my salary, but I was still scared. I couldn't fathom a future where I was reliant on myself and not a boss or stable company. What if it all disappeared? I knew that once I left my industry to do something completely unrelated it would be extremely difficult to ever go back. I wondered what my parents would think, what the bank would think, what my friends and colleagues would think. But the numbers didn't lie. I could see this was a viable business. I didn't know what the future was going to hold, but something told me that if I was smart about this, I could make it work.

Not just a leap of faith

I'm a fairly risk-averse person, and I like to make calculated decisions. Leaving a stable job to build my business online was not done on a whim. But I could see my revenue growing more and more. My calculations, based on the data that I had, indicated that I would continue to grow in the future. Planning for the next five years, I weighed up the pros and cons for pursuing my business, or staying in my City career. My business won. I made the decision then to become a full-time YouTuber (more on exactly how I got there later). Even now, I find it amazing – crazy, even! – that I was able to turn my secret hobby into my business. It came from a genuine place of passion and love, with no expectation of financial gain. When I first started there wasn't even the option to make money in this industry. But I realised I could build a long-term future doing something I was happy to work on day, night and weekends, for ever and ever.

Finding *your* grind

You might be thinking, *What exactly am I going to do if I want to go it alone? I'd better follow my passion, right?* That's what you hear all the time. But hold up a second. Because …

Passion isn't everything

What's your passion? Speaking candidly, I'd confess that my passions are sleeping in late, watching TV and eating food. I'd watch Netflix all day if I could! But you can't make a living watching telly (let's call the guys on *Gogglebox* the exception that proves the rule). You have to find something you like to do in life, but you need to acknowledge reality at the same time. And that's a philosophy I've always followed, from choosing my first job after university to deciding to become a full-time YouTuber and influencer. That doesn't mean abandoning your dreams – in fact, it's the total opposite – but it does mean acknowledging the circumstances that you're in and which lie ahead, rather than blindly ignoring them. That's why, rather than telling you to focus on finding your passion in life, I'd say focus on finding your grind.

Here's how I see it, whether we're talking about finding a hustle IRL or building your brand online. The truth is, if you're playing to your strengths, these should really be one and the same thing. This is important. Everything that I do, from my hair-extensions business to my clothing partnerships, works in synergy with what I'm doing on YouTube and my other platforms. The growth of my businesses has been natural because I'd already found what excited me and made me want to get out of bed in the morning. In fact, pretty much everything I'm going to say now applies as much to finding your business path as finding your space in the online world.

• •

LIFE LESSON: As well as following your dreams, you want to find an equilibrium between your passion and your unique skills, while also appealing to an identifiable target market – or, if we're talking about influencers, an audience. When you've managed that, you've identified a path that could be worth exploring.

• •

Here's another way of explaining that idea. There are lots of versions out there of this Venn diagram. In the digital world I replace Market with Audience. The sweet spot in the middle? That's your grind:

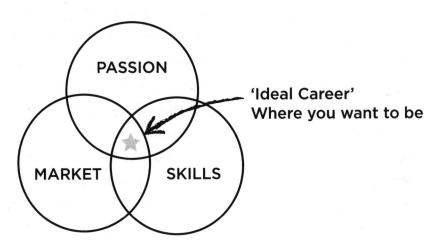

Yes, you've got to have a PASSION for what you're planning to put out into the world – you need to feel fired up, engaged, interested. What is it that sets you alight? What could you talk about for ages and not get bored? What would you be willing to dedicate all your free time (and perhaps, eventually, all your time) to? It might be making (and eating) great food. It might be running your own business. It might be being the best mother you can be. Only you know the answer. While you're at it, ignore the naysayers. People can turn up their noses at other people's interests. To that I say, who cares? Immerse yourself in what you love.

You also need to have the SKILL to back that up – that might be in the form of knowledge that you've acquired, because you're so interested in your passion you learn everything there is to know about it. It might be in terms of experience, because you've spent so many hours, days, weeks, dedicated to actually doing it. Whatever it is, it's not just a fleeting interest – you've got, or are prepared to get – the credentials. What does that look like? In my case, I was spending hours and hours on forums discovering everything I could about beauty and fashion and putting it into practise with my hustles. This was all before I started my YouTube channel, where I shared my passion for those subjects. Which meant I'd put in the time!

The third piece of the puzzle is: who's your AUDIENCE, a.k.a. your market? Does anybody else actually want to share in the thing you're passionate about? If so, who are they? Do you want to be an influencer in order to build on what you're already doing in your professional life, speaking to your peers in your industry and impressing people who could give you work? Are you speaking to consumers, who might order your product or hire you for your services? Or are you leveraging your tastes and personality to build a following of supporters who like what you're about as a person, with a view to launching a business that caters to them later on? They're all totally legitimate options, but determine what's important to you.

Once you know who your audience is, you can allow that to guide you. For example, if you have a blog aimed at fellow online business owners, it makes no sense posting photos that shout 'Look at me, I'm a bad B on the beach'. It's not related to your enterprise. Or perhaps you want to make you, as a personality, your product: do you eventually want to be able to partner with big brands, appealing to as many people as possible? Or do you only want to find a small sector of people who think exactly the same way as you – to find your tribe?

And if your audience *is* niche, and you're worried that what you want to do online seems a bit obscure, or not mainstream? That's totally fine! That's the beauty of the Internet – you might not have anyone in your town who shares your passion for say, shark movies, but you'll definitely find them online. You don't have to appeal to everyone: I don't. But I would rather have 100 engaged, enthusiastic followers, than 1,000 who aren't that interested.

Try out your grind

You might need to try out a few options when you're finding your grind. I'm a big believer in testing the water, be that IRL or online. You might think that something is your passion and, a little while later, realise you're done with it. For instance, you know that I used to style hair to earn money. I loved doing it, but eventually, I got to a place where I couldn't even be bothered to do my own hair, let alone other people's. My whole attitude was: *I need a break from this.* I realised that as much as I had enjoyed it in the past, styling hair wasn't something that I wanted to do for ever or even full-time. Yes, I had the skills and even the potential audience – or customers in this case – but it wasn't going to be the right grind for me. I'd thought it was something that I was really passionate about, but I certainly didn't want to go on to train to be a hairdresser.

So it's important to cast your net wide and see what sticks, and what you connect with the most. If you think you're going to spend the next five years reviewing eyelash brands online simply because you've decided there's an audience who want that content but aren't being catered for by anyone else, it's more than likely you're going to be completely bored. That is unless you can bring the passion, skills and knowledge to back that up. You'll need the willingness and enthusiasm to really explore that segment of the beauty industry, so you can become an expert – the connoisseur! – of lashes. And if you can bring all that, great! You can be the go-to girl for eyelashes – the only one whose opinion matters.

• •

LIFE LESSON: Passion alone is just one part of the equation: find the thing you'll be willing to grind on and dedicate every hour of the day to.

• •

Start off as a multi-hustler

I never tell people to just quit their jobs and start a business. In the same way, I wouldn't recommend that people with an Instagram account suddenly jack it all in to rely on their social media output as their sole source of income. If you can make that work, great, but that's putting a huge amount of pressure on you and there's a lot of risk attached. My approach was much more softly-softly. As I said, at the start I had no idea that my YouTube channel would become my career. At university it was a hobby, not a moneymaker. I still worked my weekend job and did hair as well. Later, I made a few career moves, and continued with YouTube on the side. It is totally OK to do more than one thing until you're ready to go all-in on your side hustle.

WHAT'S YOUR GRIND?

Ask yourself these four questions to help you discover your grind before you start putting yourself out there:

> What could you talk about every day and not get sick of?

_____

_____

_____

_____

_____

> What would you do, or be interested in, even if you didn't make a penny from it?

_____

_____

_____

_____

_____

> What are you doing or do you know about already that you could potentially share with others?

_____

_____

_____

_____

_____

> What could you keep on doing, without it feeling like a chore?

_____

_____

_____

_____

Once you've figured out your grind, that's when you can start identifying your personal goals.

In the next few chapters we'll be exploring how you can build your influence to help you achieve those goals. We'll be looking at the ins and outs of social media, building and owning a profile and honing your content. Ever wondered about embarking on the influencer journey, or growing a brand online? Read on …

3 | The importance of building a following on social media

The joy of building an online presence is that you get to share what you're doing with people all over the world. Admittedly, it can be very daunting at first. When you start out online, you can wonder if anyone's even listening, or if they care. So before you psych yourself out, I'm going to spill the tea on how I built a following and all you need to know about establishing your profile (and becoming an influencer, if that's what you want) from scratch.

The year one thousand

Ya girl hit a million followers on YouTube in January 2017. Thinking back, I still pinch myself; it was an amazing moment, but amid all the excitement I still couldn't quite fathom how I had got there. What that figure doesn't reveal is the years of hard work behind that milestone. During that time, it sometimes seemed as if some people out there could start a channel from scratch and then … boom! Six months later they had got to a million subscribers already. I wasn't sure how they had done it but, to be honest, it wasn't a priority for me. I was focused on just creating what I wanted to create.

In fact, when I first started, there were no goals for me in terms of subscribers, and there were no YouTube 'superstars'. I loved all things fashion and beauty, and I loved talking about them with other girls on forums. For me, going on to YouTube to talk about these things with even more people was just the logical next step. That didn't mean I was instantly successful. It took a long time, just like most success stories do (yes, including the 'overnight' ones). It took me a whole year to get to my first 1,000 subscribers when I started out. And I had at least 150 videos out in the world before I had 10,000 subscribers. In a way, that was perfect: there was no pressure for me when it came to the numbers game. Instead, my challenge was to find my voice, learn how to create content for those that wanted to watch, and to keep making it better.

Momentum to a million

Soon after hitting 1 million subscribers I was on track for another million: I had picked up momentum and I was on a roll. In life, everyone has peaks where you're fired up with enthusiasm, and troughs where you feel like you're coasting, and that success gave me the boost I needed at the time. While it can take a long time to feel that momentum, once you've got it, it can propel you along a monumental trajectory. In my case, it took me seven years to get to 1 million subscribers, so you might have thought it would take at least another three to achieve the same again. Wrong. One year on and I'd increased my overall following by another 1.5 million, releasing products and working with more brands in the process.

I can't tell you that building a presence in the world of social media is quick – that it's easy. It isn't. For me, the key ingredients have been heart, consistency, discipline and focus, to the point almost of obsession. It sounds super simple – and it really is – but what can make it hard is the application. The truth is, as with many things in life, a lot of us know what to do, but to actually get up, be consistent and follow up – that's the challenge we must rise to.

The value of establishing a profile

I've made YouTube the foundation of my career, while you may want to do something totally different. However, I really do believe that pretty much everyone can benefit from building a personal brand online if they wish to: it's a digital footprint that gives a positive impression of what you're about to everyone you may or may not have met, but who one day might turn into a customer, client, employer, friend (or, yes, even a lover – I see you sliding into those DMs!). Maybe your ultimate goal isn't to become an 'influencer', and that's absolutely fine! That's my hustle, but it doesn't have to be yours. Regardless, there is merit in nurturing a positive virtual reputation that precedes you.

Similarly, being an influencer doesn't have to mean being a social media star with millions of followers, or even that your platform of choice becomes your main source of income. You can have a few thousand Twitter followers, say, the majority being from your own industry, and still be influential. You can use your online presence as a way to put yourself ahead of the competition, attract attention and build your profile or product in your sector. You're building a brand. And, to do that, here's what you need to know.

You're already an influencer

If I'm honest, the term 'influencer' makes me cringe. These days it brings to mind a whole host of associations, not all of them good. Yes, I happen to take photos and film content, and people might happen to like the things I wear, the products I try, or the things I do in those photos and videos, so by default I have influence … But if you really think about it, everyone's an influencer or – the term I prefer – an 'opinion-sharer'. (Doesn't quite have the same ring to it, I know!) If you ever say, 'Mum, you look amazing in that dress', or if you tell your friends, 'I just bought this from ASOS. Do you love it?' you're already asserting your influence, shaping others' opinions. It's just what people do naturally: share what they're excited about – a great restaurant they've visited, a piece of work they're really proud of, a workout they've just smashed, or an amazing book they've just read – with other people, and update them on what's going on in their lives. So we are all influencers, be that micro or macro. And, in the social media age, more and more of us are able to generate an income through that, as well as using it to help build our businesses.

So if everyone's an influencer, you might ask, *why do it online?* The rise of social media has created a generation that lives online as well as offline – on average, we spend just over one day each week online.[1] We meet people on the Internet and what happens there increasingly feeds into and shapes our 'real life'. With that in mind, it's a no-brainer that killing it in the world of social media can really help you build your brand. But a word of caution:

---

1 Twenty-five hours each week, Ofcom figures quoted: http://www.wired.co.uk/article/uk-spends-more-time-online-sleeping

offline matters just as much. I've seen this even in my own industry, where someone might have a relatively modest following online, but they have a great real-life network that opens them up to a whole roster of invaluable online opportunities because of how they conduct themselves offline. They show up, they turn up, they talk the talk, and they present themselves well, which makes them attractive to work with.

What your influence can do for you

As I've experienced, there are more than just one or two people who wonder if this is actually a job, and if people really make a living from what I do. So I'll say it louder for the people at the back. The simple answer is: *Yes, and yes*. I'm lucky enough that I've been able to make my living from my social media platforms, as well as build businesses using the income from my platforms, all the while doing what I love. But I want to stress that the financial reward doesn't have to be the primary goal when it comes to building a following on social media. In fact it's very easy to smell from a mile off those who are in it just for the $$$. They don't usually stay round for long, as it can be a slog. I gave up my weekends and my evenings to work on my YouTube channel not with the expectation of money, but because I enjoyed it. Then, eventually, I realised, 'OK, there's an opportunity here.'

In a similar vein, while becoming an influencer, and building a brand and following, may lead to financial gain, other unexpected benefits could come your way. Yes, you can make money through traditional means like advertising and sponsorship. But there are so many other ways that you can 'win' that aren't monetary. For instance, what do you want to do in life? Do you want to be a writer, a model, an artist, a chef? You're in a position where you can showcase your skills and your work online. If what you're putting out there gets shared by others, there's more chance that people who need your services will see what you can do.

Take Rupi Kaur, one of the 'Instapoets' bringing poetry to a new audience: her first book, published in 2015, has sold 1.5 million copies and counting. Or Anok Yai, the teenager who was snapped up by a global modelling agency after an Instagram photo sent her viral. Or the Kaplan Twins, the artist sisters who have found a global audience for their creations and are the next big thing in the art world after finding fame on social media. Or Miguel Barclay, the Instagram chef whose £1 meals secured him a publishing deal to put out his own cookbook. The list goes on and on …

And those are just the ones who we hear about. There are countless people whose influence online is helping them build their network, make an impression on the world and find opportunities. Your profile online can act like a CV these days, so use it effectively to showcase what you want your personal brand to be about: the online footprint is real. We've all seen people doing things online that could limit them in life. Conversely, your presence online can be a shining representation of you and what you can do for the world. So put your best self forward!

Another thing. Think that all this is something you can sort out when you're more established and busy running your empire? Don't. It's important to build a strong online personal brand if you're still at the early stage of starting a side hustle or adding another string to your bow. You want to be able to advertise your side hustle to people who are interested in who you are and what you do – who already want to be connected to you – and increase the chances of strangers discovering you, too. All of this is more likely if you build a solid personal brand online.

And one more thing. My career has offered me something incredible. It has brought to my life something that I didn't even know was missing. I've always been a creative person but, as you've read, I almost ran away from that aspect of my personality. I wasn't confident in my ability to make a living by following that path. I believed that creative careers weren't going to provide me with the future I wanted. But my desire to be creative never left me. And, although I initially embarked on a career in the City, I was able to nurture my YouTube channel as a sideline to scratch that itch.

Even when I was working until midnight in an office, or had a pushy client on my tail, every free evening and weekend was an opportunity to be creative. For me, making each video offered me a moment where I could just breathe. This was the way I made myself happy. It was never the plan for this to be my business. I was going to be a City girl for the next thirty years! But once I realised I could turn this into a grind, it was game-on every weekend. And now, I've turned what made me happy into my job. That's why, even if I didn't make a penny from it and went back to the nine to five, I'd still make content.

That's what it's meant to me. And I'd love you to be able to tap into your creativity, enjoy this release, and connect with other people just as I have. Building a brand online might bring you other benefits that are totally different to, but just as amazing as, those I've enjoyed. You won't know until you try.

... And for the world! (Yes, really)

To me, the whole point of influence is sharing what's naturally within yourself – your thoughts, your interests, and your expertise – with which someone else can connect. Of course there are always people who want to be famous simply for the sake of being famous. But I believe any influence you wield should come from a place of genuine passion (with some caveats, as I explained with the Venn diagram on page 43). That's really important to me and should be to anyone thinking about embarking on this journey.

Don't just try to be an influencer on social media because you want to make money or promote yourself. Be an influencer because you have something interesting to say, or something to share, knowledge to impart, or something else of value to offer. If you can add value to someone or something you will always be successful. It may sound counterintuitive to take your focus off the cash and self-promotion aspect of building your online brand. But it's an attitude that I've adopted in every aspect of my work and it's served me well.

In my case, I share videos and photos of clothes, makeup, holidays, my family life – you know the drill. But, more than that, I want to share good vibes and uplift people. I see it like this: say, I post a video where I show off the latest clothes I've bought. There will be a girl who's watching who, for 10 minutes, is able to forget about some of the problems she's dealing with: a bad day at work, or the pile of coursework that's swallowing her evening. It could be as simple as me making just one viewer laugh (they tell me I'm the queen of the one-liner). She feels my positive vibes! Or perhaps someone might be looking for a job and has been rejected for several roles already and is feeling a bit down. Maybe she hears my story of how I've been made redundant in the past, and survived. Just knowing that someone else has been through something similar and lived to rise and thrive can give someone the boost they need to keep going. So, even though I believe becoming a person of influence online will help you, that's far from the only goal. Let's uplift others too.

• •

LIFE LESSON: Don't seek popularity – and this goes for online or IRL – just for the sake of being popular or promoting yourself. What *value* can you add? That's what's important.

• •

The rules of the game

Before we get into the nitty-gritty, a few rules to help you grow your following:

1   CONTENT IS KING

This might sound obvious, but it's surprising how often it's over-looked. Before all the fancy cameras, titles, lighting and editing, what a piece of content is about, how it connects to the audience or what it offers the viewer is always the most important thing to think about. I like to put myself in the shoes of the viewer and ask myself: Why would I watch this? How is it going to help the viewer, encourage or entertain them?

2   SHOW UP

When I talk about consistency, I mean two things. 1) To *regularly* post new content, rather than going weeks, even months, before putting out something new. 2) Particularly when you're starting out, it helps to be *consistent* with the type of content you're putting out, so people have a chance to understand who you are and what you bring to the table. If you're switching it up every other week, from, say, 10-minute clothing hauls to lessons in how to cook on a student budget, they're just not going to know what they're tuning into.

3   BE LIKE MADONNA

Once you've carved out an identity and a space for yourself, that's the time to think about evolving and changing – in fact, it's a necessity. You have to keep innovating to stay relevant and move with the times, like Madonna! She's always been a real chameleon: you never know when she's going to switch it up. She has stayed relevant through the decades because of her ability to change it up, push boundaries and not be a bore. In the same way, I value change, rather than sticking to a formula. Eight years in, if I was still doing the exact same thing in the exact same way as when I began, then I wouldn't be where I am now. When I started, I was really focused on hair and beauty. Then I began doing shopping hauls, DIY tutorials, reviewing clothes and, along the way, I've let people into my personal and family life too.

You will evolve and change as an individual, too. That's a

good thing, and you'll want that to be reflected in your content. Growth and progression are essential parts of a successful life. One of the most important moments in my own evolution was the decision I made to change my name online from BritPopPrincess to Patricia Bright. When I joined YouTube, it was a bit like when you picked your first email name (I don't even know what mine was, misspretty-something, something awful!). That wave of us who started on the platform back then all had random made-up names relating to how we wanted to be identified. In my case, I wanted to let people know I was British, and I was a pop fan and a princess, so that was it! Then, as I grew older, and more mature, that original name didn't feel quite so right for me. People grow on platforms, just as we do offline. We grow up, we experience life, and that's reflected in our online presence and brand. Rather than being viewed negatively, this should be celebrated and encouraged.

4   FIND YOUR VOICE

Finding your voice on social media – the tone and style that you're going to use to express yourself – is really important. It's how people are going to know you and *why* they will want to know you. Online, aim to be who you are in real life – but better! I don't see anything wrong with showing the best version of your-self online, so long as it's still authentically you. Trying to be something that you're not is a recipe for disaster as, trust me, the facade never lasts and people will eventually see right through it. In my case, my common voice – the personality that comes through regardless of what platform you find me on – is that of a girls' girl. I'm not a makeup artist and I'm not a fashion stylist, and I'll never pretend to be an 'expert', but I am someone who is friendly, approachable, uplifting, and (I hope!) funny too.

Of course, we can all be a bit of everything. Some days I'm feeling excited, some days I'm feeling inspired ... or emotional ... or lovey-dovey ... that's life. But, if I expressed my mood or emotions every time I posted a video or a picture, that could feel a bit up and down on social media. You do want variety in what you're putting out there, but at the same time you need some balance so that people know what they're going to find when they search for you online.

5 YOU DON'T NEED TO BE YOUR CONTENT

Contrary to what a lot of people might think, being an influencer doesn't mean that you have to be a 'personality', or the most attractive, or perfect-bodied individual. You don't even have to reveal your face, your name or your identity online in any way, if that's not what you feel comfortable with. Smarts and creativity trump appearances all day, every day!

In fact, there are thousands of successful feeds that never, or rarely, feature the person behind it. Some of the biggest influencers in the world do just that. Huda Beauty, who I love, and who has always been about showcasing other people's amazing makeup skills and looks and only occasionally her own. Or, you've someone like Josh Ostrovsky, a.k.a. @TheFatJewish on Instagram, who reposts memes and jokes online and adds his own original funny commentary. You can become hugely successful by reposting other people's content – and before you start shaking your head, I don't mean pulling other people's stuff uncredited and passing it off as your own! But if you've got a great eye, or an hysterical sense of humour, or amazing taste in clothes, you could focus on using that to find and repost great content that already exists. This is a great option for someone who is tight for time, and doesn't want to shoot their own photos and videos, or if you're particularly shy. (Of course, it's important to always ensure that due credit is given to the original creator and permission is sought.)

The key thing is to add value – like funny commentary, or curation. Just the fact that you're curating great content in one easy feed for your followers so they don't need to go hunting for it themselves means you're adding serious value. But you don't have to reinvent the wheel. You could always do more of your own original content when your life allows: sometimes you have to be a bit guerrilla to start off with and then switch it up. (But, if you want to avoid a car crash in the comments, always credit and link back to the original creators. That's just manners.) Similarly, there are great companies online whose feeds people love to follow, from Missguided to La Mer, and very few of those followers will know who owns each particular company. You don't have to do things the way that everybody else is doing it. You don't have to be a 'personality'.

6   IT'S OK FOR THINGS NOT TO BE OK

I've found that people respond best to honesty, candidness and openness. Whether I'm talking about my life, about clothes, about makeup, my followers don't want me to adopt a fake persona where I pretend that everything's amazing all of the time. They really can't handle that and, more than that, they're not buying it! Their attitude is, 'Tell the truth, Patricia!' They want your honest responses to what's going on: 'I'm having the worst day today' or

'That was amazing'. Then, when you do love something, they can trust that response to be genuine.

7   THINK BEFORE A TWEETSTORM

You do have to be really aware about what you put out in the digital ether. Once you begin to get known in the social space, like it or not people will be watching, clocking your movements, your opinions, what you stand for, or looking to see if you've ever said anything uncalled for. Yes, I've been dragged on Twitter, but no one has been able to drag me for anything I've said before I went full-time on YouTube because 1) I never really used Twitter that much! and 2) luckily, I haven't said anything *too* out of line.

Of course all of us have had our moments when we've said something uncalled for – a bit of a bitchy comment about someone who annoys us, or whatever – but there are certain things that you should keep offline. Because social media is not a private forum, as intimate as it can sometimes feel. It's a very big, very public world, and if people could be upset or offended by something you've said, even if it was a comment for the benefit of a friend or someone else who 'got' what you meant, the chances are, eventually, someone's going to notice.

8   WHY HATERS SIGNAL SUCCESS

I don't remember the first time I got a nasty comment online. But I do know that with success comes that kind of unwanted attention. Often, it's coming from individuals who don't know you at all. A lot of them just want to be in your position, and their comments are motivated by how they're feeling about themselves. Either way, those comments aren't something you need to take on board. It's not great for your mental health or your confidence. Delete and block them: that's the rule. Sometimes I don't block them, I just mute! They don't know they've been blocked, so they can keep on waffling to themselves and you don't have to see any of it. They're only wasting their own time. And don't search it out – because I know people do that! Some even have Google alerts on what people are saying about them, but that's a sure-fire way of inviting negativity into your day.

9   SWITCH IT UP, DON'T GIVE UP

When you're starting out, don't be afraid to ask for help. Don't be afraid to ask someone to share your content or your product if it's good. People ask me and I'm happy to do so if I like what someone's doing. For instance, smaller brands that don't have much money to advertise will get in touch to ask me if I'll consider featuring one of their products. And if I'm a fan, I'll happily do so. But if, after a few months, you're still not seeing traction – whatever that means for you – it's time to switch up your strategy. Be honest with yourself: are you producing the best possible content? Are you really connecting with your subject matter? Are you posting consistently and frequently? Tweak what you're doing – see what works – and then tweak a little more, paying attention to the reaction you're getting online.

Because, as I'll explain in the next chapter, you really do have to put your heart into it …

4 | The science bit – practical advice for building up a social media profile

Good content comes from the heart – it invokes a feeling or an emotion. Be it an image, words or video, it will make you feel a certain way: inspired, entertained, stimulated. I believe that you achieve that by creating content that relates to your audience but also relates to you – to what's important in your life. That way, you're connecting emotionally to what you're putting out there. Take, for instance, someone like Kanye West – as much as some people can't stand him and some people love him, he shares from his heart: he shares what he thinks and what he feels on social media without much of a filter, which makes him an emotive figure. That doesn't mean you have to become some sort of online provocateur! That's not me either, but I still produce the content that interests and engages me, as well as my audience. I've a genuine interest in the things I talk about, I get honestly excited by new releases and laugh at hauls that go wrong, and people can feel that.

These days, in this world of social media, you hear a lot about engagement ratio, which looks at how many followers you have versus how many likes or views you accumulate. You might have 10 million followers, but only 1 per cent of those followers actually interact with you. The way to improve engagement is to allow people to feel connected to you – and that means having an emotional relationship with your audience through the content that you create. We all know there are those who post just because they're making money and it's on their schedule, while there are others who you can tell really *feel* what they're delivering. That authenticity is what you want to capture, and there are practical things you can do to help capture that authenticity that I've learned along the way.

Creation is constant

I produce ideas almost every day, and every time I have an idea, I write it down. The other night, for instance, I thought, *I could go shopping for clothes online with a glass of wine, and see if I'm a bit freer in my choices. I could start a series: 'Tipsy shopping with Patricia'!* I sent myself a reminder, as I always do via email or text, so that I could drop it into my ideas folder later. Doing this means I can draw on all my ideas as and when I need them.

In my view, every idea is a good idea – you might not actually execute it, but at least you've got your creative juices flowing and you're open to inspiration. I often find myself inspired when I look at social media: I'll see people wearing certain items, and going to certain places, be that restaurants or holiday destinations, and that'll get me thinking. I'm just as inspired when I'm out and about – by my interactions, by travel, by the people I meet and see. If you're always scrolling through timelines and feeds, then you're not accessing all the inspiration available from just living in the world. Live life!

That's not all I do though. There can be a misconception that ideas just come to you – that you experience a *eureka* moment – and that's great when that happens, but it's not always the case. I put effort and thought into actively coming up with new ideas. For me, responding to seasonal trends and events in the calendar is key. Christmas, Valentine's – I see these as old conversations to be had again with a new perspective. Autumn, winter, going back to college, holiday season – these are the markers that shape our lives. Identify which particular trends are important to you or your audience: if you've a food blog, you can schedule content around *The Great British Bake Off* when everyone's searching for baking recipes, for instance. For me, new product releases and the launch of new ranges are always on my radar. I also put a day a week aside to brainstorm and research ideas. If I want to create great content, it is going to take more than just a quick think. Here are a few key tips to help to focus your creativity:

> Identify the events and dates that are relevant to you and your audience – a wall calendar or spreadsheet will work – something you can easily keep updated and check with a glance when you're looking for inspiration.

> Remember, inspiration is everywhere! Get into the habit of writing things down: sights, smells, sounds, whatever appeals and might get your creative juices flowing. Just get it written down.

> Set aside time to allow inspiration to come to you. Find a quiet spot and a moment where you're able to do nothing but think about your ideas.

Nothing is really new

Although I've just spent the last few paragraphs enforcing the notion of constant idea creation, at the same time, when you drill down, there's really nothing new under the sun. And that's OK! People might think they're doing something exceptionally innovative, but it's more likely they're improving on something that's been done before – and there is absolutely nothing wrong with that! If you can identify a problem with someone else's service, brand or business model, you can put your own spin on it. People want choice, they want options, and they are always on the lookout for something that might suit them better than what is already out there.

Take the ridiculously amazing launch by Fenty Beauty, the collaboration between superstar Rihanna and beauty-brand developer Kendo. The makeup brand completely disrupted the beauty industry by putting the spotlight on diversity: *Time* magazine even named it one of the most important inventions of 2017 for what they called its 'quality-to-affordability ratio and its emphasis on inclusivity'. That September, one of the Pro Filt'r Soft Matte foundations was sold every minute.[1] Yes, there were already tons of existing cosmetic brands that even sold more shades in a very crowded market – but Fenty tapped into an appetite for something fresh that wasn't being met or celebrated in the same way. The

---

1 https://graziadaily.co.uk/beauty-hair/makeup/rihanna-world/

same goes for content when you're coming up with ideas: there is always a new twist to be put on something that's already out there.

I do that all the time. For instance, I saw people doing first-impression makeup videos, trying out new makeup products for the very first time and sharing their reactions. I realised that I could do the same thing, but for fashion. I started to give my first impressions of clothes I'd bought, straight out of the box they'd arrived in. At the time, people tended to only show the items they really liked and never shared anything that didn't look so good: 'I love this. I love this. I love this.' What I wanted was to show the process we all go through before that stage, when we buy things online. The truth is that for every ASOS order I make, I probably only keep a couple of pieces. I wanted to share the process around that, where I realise that something I thought would look great doesn't suit me at all, and give my honest first impression. That was my own twist I put on something that was already out there and now it's a staple on my channel.

. . . .

LIFE LESSON: I have no problem with copying but – and this is important – you have to copy and innovate. Always bring something fresh to it.

. . . .

Plan, plan, plan

It's one thing to stay creative and come up with ideas; staying on top of your output is another matter. As ever, I love to be organised. If the first step is brainstorming ideas, the next is planning. On a practical level, I would always recommend setting out a content plan, to organise your thoughts on what you want to put out into the world. In my case, I have a number of beautiful Excel spreadsheets (thanks to my consulting days, I'm a whizz at Excel) that I use to set out what content I'm going to create, and which platform I'm going to put it out on. It's all about taking the time to:

> Think about what's important to the season.
> Think about what's important to me.
> Think about what my audience would want.
> Map that out into a schedule.

I do this every month, focusing on my YouTube and Instagram, but you could pick whichever platforms appeal to you. I'll pick ideas that I've already brainstormed and noted down in my folder, and plug them into this content plan. I'll also 'goal match' – check my plan against my goals. Let me explain: I have another document, an Excel spreadsheet (surprise, surprise), where I set goals for my content each month. I say goals, but they are broader than that: really they are content strands, such as beauty, fashion or hair. I will also list my personal goals, so if I am working on a particular project, I will plan content relating to its launch or release to get people excited. I always want to balance my content so it doesn't become too focused on one element or 'goal': so, I might plan to film a fashion video on Monday, where I review my latest high street haul; a beauty video on Wednesday, where I try out a particular cosmetics range; then on Saturday, I might do a video Q&A, answering people's questions and offering a bit of encouragement. Variety is the spice of life, after all – for me and my audience. I check in with my goals every few months, making sure that I am making content that is aligned with what I want to do as a person.

My content plan also details my edit schedule – setting time aside to edit my videos and photos – and my upload schedule. That means I will know on Saturday I'm going to film a certain video and that I will post it the following Monday. In all honesty, the time and day isn't that important – but having a plan is. I really do recommend that you do the same. You know what they say about failing to plan … Here's an example of what a content plan might look like:

Ideas
When you feel ugly
Dried prune booty hacks
Reacting to celeb outfits
Mukbang + Q&A

Goals	
Considerations	**Notes**
Fashion Week	
Bake Off seasons	Inspired by cakes
Black Fridays	Amazon discounts

Content Schedule		
Edit date	**Upload date**	**The Big Idea**
10 Aug	13 Aug	Pinterest clothing hacks
10 Aug	15 Aug	Trying new beauty trends
13 Aug	18 Aug	What it's like being a mum

Rise above your platform

I want to speak about platforms for a second: I know people wonder which is the best one to focus on. The answer is: the one that suits your content. Are you a great writer? Start a blog. Love cracking one-liners? Try Twitter. Do you love images, and taking photos? Head to Instagram. You have to work out what works for you. Personally, I like to talk – clearly! – so that's why I found YouTube the perfect outlet to share what I thought was important. Today, I'm a fan of using as many platforms as you can, within reason – you want to be able to deliver good content on every one you're using.

That said, you can't be wedded to one platform, because things change. Myspace was once the biggest social-networking site in the world – and now it's not. (And the biggest today? That could already have changed by the time you read this.) Being able to be fluid is important. At times, I've found that I've been sceptical and so late to join a platform, then eventually fallen in love with it. However, being on the newest platforms as they take off can really help you pick up momentum at the start. Yes, they might also fail, but sometimes it's worth taking a gamble! Think about it – the field is open, so it's easier to get attention when people are still discovering who's who on a particular platform. I'm speaking from experience: I was on YouTube before it was as big as it is today. Being an early adopter of a platform can make a big difference.

Whatever platforms you do use, put everything under the same name as much as possible. These days, I'm Patricia Bright on all my platforms so that if someone searches for me, they find all the good stuff! Likewise, when you start to get mentions about you or your brand in articles, doing interviews, getting into the press, all of this will support your online footprint, building awareness of what you're up to. As you're establishing yourself, you may also want to consider bagging a website with you or your brand's name. It's simple: you go to a domain seller like Namecheap.com or GoDaddy.com (there's lots of them) to register your name and pay an annual fee to keep it. You may not have use for it (or so you may think) right at the start, but you never know where your name could take you, so it makes sense to own it – the sky's the limit, after all! Down the line, you can use a website builder like Wix or Squarespace that offers lots of easy templates for you to build the site itself. Someone's got the website address already? You're in good company! Someone else has bagged patriciabright. com – she's a psychologist. It doesn't bother me. I just went for patriciabright.co.uk instead.

All the gear and no idea

You don't need to spend loads of money on high-end equipment to produce good content. I watch people who are so engaging that I'm completely absorbed in what they're saying – never mind that their lighting isn't perfect. Equally, you can have all the gear and be boring as hell! Audiences care about you rather than your lighting.

In practical terms, that means you don't need a fancy camera if you want to film or post pictures, particularly as you get started. You just need the camera on your smartphone, and some editing software. My favourite photo-editing apps are VSCO Cam and Snapseed – I don't use any other filters. I also rely on Final Cut Pro and Adobe premiere, which is for video editing. When I began filming, natural lighting worked really well for me. I'll be honest, it can be changeable at times, but the result can be beautiful when you pick the right moment. For some added enhancement and to give you some extra light, you can buy umbrella lighting from Amazon for about £60.

If you're in a position where you feel like you need to develop stuff a little further for you or your business's needs, consider finding someone to teach you. If I look back on my output from five years ago, it's gone from grainy and out of focus to looking a lot more professional. It's been a learning curve, but everything can be learned on Google and YouTube – I taught myself a lot that way, from which camera settings to use, to how to add a blur effect to images. But I also had someone teach me how to use Photoshop; I use PeoplePerHour, where I can hire freelancers with expertise in a certain area.

• •

LIFE LESSON: You don't have to be the expert in everything. Find the people with the skills you need, whether you're starting out or are recruiting for your empire!

• •

Done is better than perfect

I still always feel nervous when I shoot a video: I almost have butterflies, thinking, *Are people going to like this? Am I making sense?* Every single time, even now, I wonder, *Is this any good?*

And I know that staying a little bit nervous is good. (In fact, research shows nerves can give you the boost you need to excel: athletes do best when they're experiencing both negative and positive feelings.[1] In other words, being too relaxed isn't always ideal …) Yet while it's important to have high standards, and I will always keep pushing myself, I've realised that perfectionism will actually stifle you. I know people who want what they deliver to be so amazing that they end up putting nothing out there at all, because nothing's ever good enough. There's always some imperfection if you look for it. Anyhow, the truth is, you are not necessarily the best judge of a piece of content. On occasions, I've produced content that I wasn't entirely sure about, and had an amazing response. Conversely, a video that I thought was perfect might turn out to not be that perfect in my audience's eyes! Perfection is determined by the audience or the customer.

Generally speaking, in life more broadly I don't aspire to be a perfectionist. I'm not. I view success as a series of iterations. Something new like a YouTube channel can start out iffy, a bit shoddy, but with time and practice it gradually gets better and better, the audience becomes more engaged, and eventually it's amazing. But you cannot expect to start at the top of your game. Recently, I've been working on a clothing brand. When I look at my first designs compared to my current styles, I'm shocked, thinking, *These are already so different.* Even the software that we used to create them has upgraded! And I'm still learning. I might come out with just a few really good pieces, and then my next collection will be even bigger and better, as I grow and learn.

---

1 www.self.com/story/how-to-make-your-anxiety-work-for-you-instead-of-against-you

• •

LIFE LESSON: They say it takes ten years to make
an overnight success. Everything is about the little
changes, the small steps forward, when no one is
looking. So enjoy them …

• •

Build your audience in 10 minutes a day (plus a Saturday afternoon)

So after all that I hope you're not feeling daunted? No? Good?
Now let's explore creating a routine.

Put a plan in place for your social media strategy. By that, I
mean looking at your schedule, putting time aside to invest in
what you want to do, from taking photographs to editing them,
and from writing a blog post to brainstorming ideas for new
content. Maybe you've got a nine to five, and think you don't
have the time. But you do. Here's the secret.

Spend 10 minutes a day on your social media – and
kill it on the weekend

Every day, in your lunch break or after work, you can spend
around 10 minutes to have a think about and prepare what you're
going to do when you've an entire day or afternoon to play with.
That means that when the weekend finally arrives, you're not
thinking, *What should I do today?* Instead, you wake up and
you're ready. I did this myself: at my busiest, during my stint in

the City when I was working till midnight in the office (more on that later), my YouTube channel became something that I had to save until the weekend. It was how I would relax after working intensely all week. But I was still thinking about videos during the working week and getting excited about my ideas. At lunch-time, for instance, I would go into Boots and see what products I could find that might make a video at the weekend. It wasn't a chore – it was an exciting way of preparing and planning for my content.

HOW TO USE YOUR TIME

What your 10 minutes a day for five days a week is going to do, is lay the preparation for three to four solid hours of work at the weekend – minimum. First, pick what you're going to focus on. When you're trying to start out, don't try and do everything all at once. You can't. Think. Is it a video you want to put out this week? Is it a beautiful image you want to create? And then break it down, step by step.

Say, my goal for the week is to take a photo in a red dress near St Paul's, the famous cathedral in London, with a gorgeous city-scape behind me – that's my idea. There are all sorts of ways I can use my 10 minutes a day to prep for that before the weekend rolls around. It might be finding that gorgeous red dress online. It might be scrolling through all the hashtags relating to St Paul's on Instagram to find the best vantage point before I even get there. It might be compiling a list of relevant hashtags so that I'm prepared when I post my image, ready to go. It might be deciding how I'm going to pose and what type of image I want: I actually keep screenshots of people's poses that I like, and refer to them when

I'm feeling a bit awkward. You have to learn from somewhere, right?! If you're starting out, it might be using 10 minutes to practise using a photo-editing app on some stock images, so that when you capture your image, you know what to do to make it look just as you want. You might arrange to meet the person who's going to take the photo. Then on Saturday morning, all you've got to do is get to the spot you've already picked, and take your shots!

The same principle applies whatever the medium. For example, if you want to film a video at the weekend, spend 10 minutes in the week thinking about what you want to do in your video. Take another 10 minutes to research the idea. Then 10 minutes to check you've everything you need, and if you have to order or buy anything to include. You can use another 10 minutes to jot down notes on what you want to say. I like to write bullet points before I start talking, because if not, I go round the houses on various tangents and lose focus. So, when Saturday comes around you're not going to be sitting there unsure about what to do or say. As you get more practised, you could aim to film two videos on the weekend if you've an afternoon spare; three if you've more time. Then, in the following week, you could do 10 minutes of editing on Monday or Tuesday before you post each video, if you ran out of time at the weekend. I'm not worried about *what* exactly you're doing in those 10 minutes every day. It's about getting into the habit of making this part of your life, and something that you engage with even when things get busy.

These days, it takes me two to three hours to film a YouTube video, including set-up. I get my monitor ready so I can see myself and what's in frame; the room gets really hot from the lights, so I set up a fan. I make sure my camera batteries are charged and my memory cards are cleared so I won't run into problems. I lay out any products I want to talk about and take a few minutes to just centre myself and make sure I'm in the right headspace, ready to film. Many a time I've shot a video where it looks like I captured it all in my first attempt, but in fact I shot it three or four times. Perhaps I didn't like what I was saying, maybe I didn't feel I presented it well enough, or perhaps I noticed my hair was sticking up. It could be something trivial or something crucial, but the outcome's the same – I'll sit down and reshoot. I've tried to do that less, and not to judge myself so much. There are videos of me out there that I look back on that to the viewer seem seamless, but so much effort went into them. It's part of the process.

- -

LIFE LESSON: Go all in on a project in terms of your energy and dedication. If you've one foot in, one foot out, you can't be successful in anything. Tell yourself: 'This is what I'm doing. This is how I'm doing it.' Come up with a plan – give it all you've got and execute it.

- -

What's your magic number?

You will speed up as you build up experience, but there isn't a magic number in terms of how often you should aim to create content or how much new content you post. You have to find what works for you. I would say more than once a week is ideal for YouTube, while for other social media platforms the expectation may be higher in terms of how frequently people expect you to post. That said, test your audience, find that sweet spot and stick to it. A huge YouTuber, Casey Neistat, used to only upload new content every few months, but every video would get millions of views. The quality of what he was putting out was so good that posting a video and then effectively disappearing for a while worked for him. But, he was unique – and later on even he started posting more often.

In terms of timing, I like to post new content in the evening and the morning, when people are commuting and checking their phones. You can check your analytics, offered by pretty much every platform in some form, to see what sort of time gets the best reaction. Also, ask your audience. When do they want to see new content?

So it's that simple? Not quite. That's how you're fitting it into your life. What you're putting out into the world is a different matter. And for that, you're going to turn to your most important resource – other people like YOU …

WEEK AHEAD PLAN

Use the week ahead to set your own 10-minute plan.

This week, I want to produce ...

> 10-minute task on Monday:

_____

_____

> 10-minute task on Tuesday:

_____

_____

> 10-minute task on Wednesday:

_____

_____

> 10-minute task on Thursday:

_____

_____

> 10-minute task on Friday:

_____

_____

I will keep Saturday morning/afternoon / Sunday morning/afternoon
(delete as appropriate) clear to do my:

_____

WEEKEND-TASK:

_____

Then, if needed, I will use my 10 minutes a day in the following week to

_____

Sorted! You can keep doing this every week. You're on your way.

5 | Taking your audience to the next level of growth

So far, I've been focused on what *you* need to do. Now, I want to focus on the people who allow you to go on this journey: your audience. As mentioned earlier, at the time of writing I've more than 2 million followers, which is mind-blowing when I think about it. But whether you have 10 people listening to you, or 10,000, the principles remain the same. Call them viewers, customers, clients, fans or supporters: if you are building a business, an online presence, or any kind of enterprise, you will need to carry people with you. It's a two-way relationship that really can be magical.

OK, let's address the most obvious question … how *do* you build that relationship? My number one rule here is:

Focus on your followers

That's what I try to do always: work out what my audience like, why they keep coming, why they keep staying, and then keep giving them what they like. Building an audience is about your creativity, yes, but also about thinking outside of yourself. Nowadays, I consider myself to be someone who is providing a service to my viewers. That perspective is really important, whatever you are doing in life. Don't focus just on you and your growth and development – think about the people that you impact on the other end of the screen or through your newsletter or website. As social influencers, we're creating content for people who enjoy us. So it makes sense to respond to what they want to hear from us.

You need to give your time to your audience, being very responsive and reacting to what they ask of you. When I upload a video, I will always sit there for at least an hour responding to comments, liking, and thanking people, just to let people know that I care. I find it very rewarding – I love reading their comments, good *and* bad. What I do wouldn't be anywhere near as fun if there wasn't that reaction from the crowd. As well as reading your comments, you can get scientific about gauging audience interest. I've used SurveyMonkey and other online surveys in the past, when I was about to launch a product. I wanted to know: what do my audience want, what do they spend on, what do they like, what are the key issues for them? People love to give their opinions and, whatever your business, surveys can be incredibly useful.

On a practical level, I believe my most recent growth has been driven by me taking on board the suggestions that my audience have made. Every time I've delivered on what they've requested, I have performed really well. Of course, there are some ideas that wouldn't quite work for me, but there are certain genuine gems that I feel could only come from my audience. For instance, when I started my clothing reviews, people would suggest websites that I've never heard of, such as the Wish e-commerce app. People started leaving comments telling me, 'You should try Wish', which would collect thousands of likes from my other followers. Of course I listened. Now, my review of the clothes I've bought on Wish is my most popular video, with 6 million views and counting.

And if something gets a great reaction, pay attention. I check my data and I see what videos got the most positive or the least positive response. YouTube, Instagram, Twitter all offer their own analytics or insights as a way for you to gauge your progress. Have your views gone up? Have your views gone down? Where are your subscriber numbers? When I began putting out first-impression haul videos, the response was out of this world and, moreover, I really enjoyed making this type of content, especially knowing I was producing something my audience loved, too. My audience kept responding really well to them, so I've made those videos a regular aspect of what I do.

And if something gets a bad reaction? Just put up something different afterwards and move on. If you're going to fail (and failure is an inevitable product of trying anything new) then fail fast.

• •

LIFE LESSON: I like to say that you're only as good as your last piece of work – which, when you think about it, is pretty liberating. So something you've tried hasn't gone down so well? Just make your next piece of content better! Keep improving. Keep developing. Keep challenging yourself.

• •

Grow with your base

My audience tends to be young women who, like me, love beauty and fashion and like to know what's up. However, I also come across sixty-year-old women who tell me, 'I follow you. I love you!' I've met them in person, when I'm out and about, and in my comments. So you never know who might be touched by, or connect with, something you put out into the world. As an influencer, I've shared my journey as a makeup and fashion fanatic, as a student, as an employee, as a businesswoman, and as a mum. That means different audiences can connect with various aspects of me, for which I'm very grateful.

At the same time, I have felt resistance when I've started to talk about something new. It's inevitable. Some people will love it when you try new things, while others will say, 'You've changed. Your stuff's not the same.' And of course, as I've touched on earlier, over the years you are going to change. So, as much as I say listen to your audience, ultimately you also have to balance this with doing what feels right to you too.

For instance, I had a season of not wanting to focus on fashion – I was over it. I was all about makeup and lifestyle at the time. Eventually, having had a break, I felt a renewed sense of passion to resume my fashion content, and it benefited from me having been able to wait for my genuine enthusiasm to return. In the end, it's up to you to define who you want to be – and yes, that may affect the size of your audience. It may not be the largest, if you stay true to yourself and what interests you – but it will be a dedicated audience. They'll be engaged. And that's a powerfully beautiful thing.

It's not just about the numbers …

I understand why people do it, but do not under any circumstances buy followers. There are different schemes by which you can pay for followers to make it look like your audience base is expanding – I wouldn't recommend any of them. The best way to build your audience is to create content that people truly connect with. In the long term, those quality followers matter more than any fair-weather (or even fake) followers.

… Or about the money

The bigger you get, the more opportunities you may be offered. For some, this may mean brands start to seek you out to produce sponsored content. As influencers, we really do increase awareness around brands and products that we like, and alert people that there is something amazing out there. It's a service which can be invaluable and, in a sense, has replaced traditional advertising to a large extent. However, if you are going to accept said offers, as I've mentioned, it's important to protect your integrity: stay true to what interests you, and what aligns with your values. Focus on producing content to please yourself and your audience – not any would-be sponsors. And it should go without saying, but always follow the law in relation to gifts, sponsorship and ads. It changes, so I won't attempt to explain it all here. But the fundamental rule is: disclose everything. Regulation is there for a reason; it protects the consumer. What's more, I, as a creator, prefer being up front and saying, 'This is sponsored' – I celebrate that! I'm happy and proud to work with the brands I do. That's why I will always make it clear that I've been given something or paid to do something.

Why it's good to keep moving the goalposts

I'm a 'done that. What's next?' person. I'm not very good at accepting my current success because 1) I feel like success can evaporate very quickly, and 2) the sky is the limit, for all of us. Having reached 2 million subscribers, I've realised my goal isn't necessarily growing to 10 million. Having 50 million followers won't make me any happier! I've realised that if you set a numerical or a physical goal and meet it, you're almost going to feel disappointed because you're still the exact same person you were before you met that goal.

These days, my goal is to keep growing in a much broader sense: to keep getting better and giving more. I like to reflect and check that I am doing that, and also I like to continually challenge myself. When I stop feeling challenged, I have to create or do something else. Ultimately, I want to be able to offer something to those people who follow me that will improve their lives … and mine. Because isn't that what life's really all about?

Sometimes though, it can be difficult to focus on what's important and to not get distracted by what other people are doing (or seem to be doing). So let's move on – because now I want to share all I've learned about how to thrive, staying focused on your grind, despite what happens online and IRL …

DEFINE YOUR GOALS

I want you to take a moment here to write down all your goals, as they come to you, be they short term, maybe a possibility in five years', or reaching for the stars. Take that time to really think about what you want and articulate it to yourself. You won't necessarily achieve everything you write down – if you're anything like me, your goals might change and you might end up setting aside some of the ideas you had – but take this chance to let yourself dream big, without fear of failure.

_____

_____

_____

_____

_____

_____

_____

_____

_____

_____

_____

_____

_____

_____

_____

_____

_____

_____

_____

_____

_____

6 | Online vs real life

That perfect Instagram kiss, right, the way he looks at her is #COUPLEGOALS, #IWISHMYMANWOULD … we're all guilty of having these fleeting thoughts. The reality, of course, can be very different. After all, how natural is it for two people to capture the perfect kiss every time the camera clicks? Speaking from experience, they've probably been there for 20 minutes, telling each other, 'No, you're not kissing me right!' No one knows how much squabbling was involved.

Even I have to check myself. I see people posting cute family photos, the kind of photos that I'd love to take, but half the time my child has places to go and people to see, so isn't the most eager to cooperate! If I try to take her picture, Grace will often just wriggle away. I'll ask myself, *How do people take these gorgeous photos of their children?* We all have to fight that impulse to constantly compare – and that's why I like to pull back the veil, a little bit.

Once, I was away on a trip with some other influencers, and

some had gone to bed early while I had carried on enjoying myself all night long. They were going to get up at two o'clock in the morning to take a photo at a gorgeous landmark when no one was around. That's what you call dedication to the cause. I knew that they were blurry-eyed and tired, but you couldn't tell that from their photos. It was another case of reality versus Instagram. The takeaway from all of these stories is that there are normal people with their own issues and challenges behind these images. The trick is to avoid comparing yourself to the carefully edited versions of them - all it will do is undermine your confidence. Comparison is the thief of joy, it's a distraction from your grind, and leaving it behind is just one of the many ways you can thrive in every single area of your work and life. But there are more.

How I feel about photoshop

If you capture a beautiful photo and Photoshop it (or use any other kind of picture-editing technology, which is what people often mean when they talk about Photoshop) to make it as perfect as possible, I say: go right ahead and do what makes you feel happy. In fact, sometimes I like a lot of heavily edited photos because they're appealing to my eye. I can see that someone has put an effort into making something look more beautiful, and I applaud that. Art is an illusion. Even I am not showing myself online when I am crying into my cereal bowl with my morning eye bags showing because I'm stressed out and tired! I share my life, but I don't share all of it.

At the same time, I am big advocate of unfollowing people who make you feel bad about yourself, just as, in the same way, I'd say steer clear of people who make you feel bad in real life. Yes, the feeling that you are feeling may be because of your own issues or insecurities, and nothing to do with them as a person – but do it anyway! It's fine to think: *You know what? I can't follow you any more because, honestly, it makes me a little upset.* That's a practical tip: If someone makes you feel bad, for whatever reason, unfollow. If they give off any negative energy, unfollow. Because it's far more beneficial to be totally focused on what you can contribute, not what others are up to.

Learning to say no. No. No!

When I started out, and was just beginning to get some attention on YouTube – from brands, as well as individuals – I felt under pressure to do what people asked me to do. I would say yes to deals, yes to projects, and didn't know how to say, 'No, I'm not going to do that – it's not right for me.' In the past, I've worked with brands that have been very specific and very tight in the way they wanted to sponsor my content, not allowing me to express myself in my normal way. They'd tell me to use certain words or language, and that just doesn't work for me.

Early on in my career, I filmed for a great high street brand – it was the first time a crew had filmed me – and I was interviewing people in a studio, pointing to a model. That segment went out on my channel. But my audience didn't like the content, because it wasn't what they were used to seeing. It was what the brand wanted, rather than what they or I wanted. Although I got paid, it wasn't worth doing because it devalued me.

On another occasion, I ended up shooting some content on a trip. I really wasn't happy with what I ended up with. I knew it wasn't great for my audience, but because the brand had already put all that investment into the trip and the content, I couldn't pull out at that stage. Contracts are legally binding and I couldn't afford to be sued! So I put it out. But everything about it made me cringe. And it was another lesson: I read a lot of fine print now and make sure that I am really feeling everything I say yes to. Often, if something doesn't feel right, it probably isn't right. You're never going to be proud of something that you don't really connect to.

These days, a brand might still ask me, 'Could you cut this part of the video, that was a bit too honest', but I will stand firm and say, 'No, I need to keep that in.' It's about protecting my integrity and knowing I am putting out content that I am happy with. I have also learned to say no to my audience when they make certain requests. For instance, people have always wanted to see more of my relationship and my baby, and in the past I'd feel guilty not sharing that with them. Now, I am more comfortable in saying, 'No, I need to keep parts of our lives just for us.'

• •

LIFE LESSON: However glittering it may look, steer clear of an opportunity that just doesn't feel right for you. Say no with confidence and walk away with your head held high. You have to know your own value.

• •

Tune out the haters

Someone is always going to have something to say about what you are doing, so you are going to have to trust your own voice and block out the haters. In my own case, when I had started working at the bank and my fellow interns and colleagues found out that I was shooting videos for an unknown dodgy website (or so they thought), the reaction wasn't great. I was a joke. One of my intern friends told me, 'Patricia, you know this doesn't look good, especially for this job.' The worst thing was that I knew he wasn't being mean – he was worried for me. My peers thought my hobby meant I wasn't serious about my career, that I didn't really want to get ahead at work. I cried – I'm a crier! – and I removed all my colleagues from my Facebook page. I put my channel on private so no one could see anything.

But, after a while, my perspective shifted to: *Whatever. I don't care what you all think. This is what I like doing, this is my hobby. Some people play football, others enjoy a round of golf; I make videos about makeup.* So I turned my YouTube back to live, but now I kept it on the down-low. When I'd meet work friends for lunch, someone might ask me: 'You still doing those YouTube videos?' 'Yeah, I am,' I'd say, vaguely, but I wouldn't get into just how much time I was spending on them. Luckily, they weren't really the demographic to watch: techy geek boys are not going to be looking for my beauty videos! I kept my head down, and got on with my own thing.

When online runs into IRL

It's a fact of life that some of your activities outside your job may not be viewed that favourably by your boss or colleagues, as in my case. (Do check your contract for any non-compete clauses if you're planning to launch a similar business or to see if they own the copyright to any ideas you come up with during your employment! Don't get caught out.) Does that mean don't do it? No, that's not what I'm saying. Yes, you have to be careful, but you do also have to take risks to progress in life.

Obviously, there are limits. If you're a single mum with mouths to feed, for example, I wouldn't recommend that you do anything dramatic to jeopardise your job without any back-up plan. However, you don't have to spill the beans on everything that you're working on in your own time. I never shared my YouTube presence with my bosses while I worked in the corporate world because I didn't think doing so was going to benefit me particularly. I had this secret that sustained me for years through the office grind.

That said, in many cases you can be honest with your employers and say, 'This is what I do.' And, if anything, they might be quite impressed when they realise their employee has, say, a following on social media: 'I didn't know that you did this. Show us how to do it.' In the case of one girl I know, she used to share beautiful pictures of the food she made. She was working in a marketing department for a drinks brand at the time, but the company also looked after restaurants and she was able to move into the restaurant side of the business because of the social media following she had built in the food world.

• •

LIFE LESSON: Share your stuff with pride if you see the opportunity – but never compromise your wellbeing (or your killer business idea).

• •

Boundaries and breaks

I sometimes like to share my feelings about something after the event, so I'm protected by that little bit of distance. I don't decide, consciously, what I will keep back, but of course I don't have my phone on me all the time. Before we got married, I broke up with my partner Mike, who of course is now my husband, for a year. And I remember sharing that on my channel, but I gave myself time to process what had happened before I posted it. In fact, it might be years later that I share a particular journey – and I'll do that if I feel someone is going to learn from it. If it's just to join in my drama, then there's no point. But, if you think you're strong enough to share something that's going on in your life while it's happening, share it. In my experience, most people are supportive and give love. 'Chin up, girl,' they tell me. 'Chin up.'

When I became a mum, I shared my birth experience. That was a big thing for me – a decision that I went back and forth about for a while. Eventually, I decided, *This was such a beautiful moment for me. I'm just putting that out.* I myself had watched a lot of other women's birthing videos – babies crowning, everything! – which gave me more confidence when it came to giving birth myself. That was another reason why I decided to put that video out: I felt it could help other women. Today, when it comes to my daughter, I love to capture footage of her, but there's a balance. If I felt I was filming her because I had to make a living from her, I personally wouldn't do it. Even the Kardashians, who have shared so much of their lives with the world for so long, can be quite private with their children. Remember Kylie not even confirming that she was pregnant with her baby Stormi until after she had arrived.

But everyone is different. I don't criticise those who do share a lot about their children online, but I'd suggest that even they take breaks regularly. Social media can become all-encompassing when you're always on it. Also, it's very important to learn and remember how to be bored – especially if you are a creator. It's at the times when your mind isn't getting constant feedback and stimulation that you're able to come up with fresh new ideas. So, at the weekend, I physically turn my phone off. If anybody needs me desperately, they can call my landline. We all need to allow ourselves time offline to reflect, recharge and reboot our creativity. Then, we can hit the hustle even harder.

Now, I want to turn to something that we can sometimes shy away from – but which is just as important as tapping into your creative side: how to stay on top of your money …

7| Create your wealth

Earlier, I shared with you where I came from and the events in my childhood that shaped me. My past is what put a fire in my belly and gave me my drive, but what I want to talk about here is how my experiences have also played a huge part in determining my attitude to work, my career and my finances.

Making the choice for things to be different

Growing up, I was always the kid who never had fancy jewellery or the cool stuff that it felt like all the other kids had. If my school uniform got ripped, it would be sewn and patched up and I was just going to rock with it. Having said that, the lack of money wasn't something I would ever have complained about. What was that going to do? Even then I knew that not having money isn't something that fundamentally defines who you are, and who you could be. I knew it was just my situation at that point in my life. Although it might sound cliché, I never felt poor because I was rich in spirit: I had my family and I really was very happy. But, yes, from the outside, I knew that we were what other people might define as 'poor'. And that's one of the drivers for me, even now, because as happy as I was in other ways, I wanted things to be more comfortable financially – particularly because my mum had to work so hard.

I don't linger on the past, but I wanted to share my experiences with you so you can understand why being able to look after myself financially, manage my money, be a boss, and run a successful business is all so important to me. I'm going to show you how I did it – and how taking control and knowing how to manage your money can help you build the life you want, too.

Live lavish ... But watch the pennies

Despite what appearances might suggest, I'm a saver, not a spender. It's hardwired into me to be frugal and sensible with my money, because I know what it's like to be without it. I know that's not the case for everyone – and, even though I am naturally careful, I've still managed to have my share of money headaches! Even with the best of intentions, we can start the month thinking *I'll be sensible with my money,* ready to be a boss, and by the end of it we're living off Pot Noodles and having to turn down nights out. It's normal. However, I've found it's important to learn how to have the right mindset towards saving money and putting it aside for a greater purpose. Just because you have it right now, doesn't mean you have to spend it straight away!

Why watch the pennies? Because it gives you options. It's how, as I'll explain, I've been able to fund my ideas and ventures without having to max out any credit cards, borrow from the bank or ask friends or family for money, as some start-up founders do. My saving habit allowed me to invest in my start-up, which ultimately helped me to prosper. In fact, saving, by allowing you to launch a new venture, like I did, can ultimately lead you to have more.

So, what does that save-not-spend attitude look like day-to-day?

I have a simple calculation constantly in my head: *What do I have coming in? vs What do I have going out?* I focus on paying all essentials, such as bills, mortgages, salaries and the taxman. I then see what I have left. In some people's eyes it could be 'spending money'; in my eyes that money could be used to invest in my ideas, or at least to save. For those of you wanting to start a business or build your profile, it *will* take some investment. From cameras and equipment, to marketing and product creation, building your ideas takes funds. So the sacrifices you make to put money aside will add up and make a difference in terms of you actually creating a future you want.

Even the little things we casually take for granted count. For example, food. I got to a place where I realised far too much of my money was going on eating out. I realised I could spend anywhere between £10 and £35 per day (*excluding* dinners where I eat out, at least twice a week). Realistically that amounted to over £4,000 per year. And I know I wasn't alone. Last year, 11.36 billion meals were eaten out of the home – that's 3.3 meals a week for every person in the UK.[1] But how many of those are real treats, or even necessary, rather than just the easy option? I had to learn to cut back on this, to cook at home more and not splurge as much. These days, I cook at home as often as possible,

---

1 According to market research company NPD, cited in the *Daily Mail*, 16/03/2018

making a big batch of something that I can put in the freezer: one-pot meals, chickpea stir-fries, chicken stews, with rice as an accompaniment (I always have that in the fridge). To me food is precious, but it doesn't have to break the bank. As I say, I'd rather go to Nando's than Nobu!

Travel's another area where I save. It's easy to find yourself catching a little Uber here, a little Uber there, at the tap of an app. But as much as I love the convenience, I save these for special occasions. Instead, you will find me riding around on the train or the Underground. I'm a London Transport queen! I've been caught many a time asleep on the train, mouth wide open, and then seen that someone has pulled out their phone to take a picture. (To be honest, a train sleep is one of my favourite types of nap!) Where possible, find out what discounts are available when it comes to tickets, from family travel to student offers, and if it's an option set off at a later time so you can travel off-peak.

Of course, I do have my weaknesses: you know how much I love clothes. For the most part, I'll shop at Topshop and Zara rather than designer brands, and I will hunt down bargains before clicking on that online shopping basket. I will try to search online for a discount code, or see if anyone else on Instagram is offering one for a certain website. I'm a coupon junkie! And, in terms of the big treats, I will only ever buy luxury items here and there. Of course I love a designer item as much as the next person but realise that they feel extra special when I believe I've put in the work, rather than just treating myself whenever I feel like it. I started off by only making one designer purchase a year. While still working in the City, I remember back when I bought my first-ever Prada bag. I felt like a boss, like I had earned it – because

I had! I had paid for it out of my own cash saved over the year, and the purchase wasn't an issue because I'd saved enough. Even now that I have more, I may make a few more splurges here and there, but in general I really would rather put that money in the bank, and know that I am building for the future.

One area where I am willing to spend is on experiences, as I consider the ability to learn from other people, places and cultures invaluable. Having visited more than thirty destinations, I feel that travelling has added to my life significantly. And I started exploring the world long before I had become a 'multi-hustler' and had additional money from my side hustles. From finding cheaper flight options (Monday to Wednesday is usually the cheapest time to fly, while weekends are almost always the most expensive),[1] to staying in luxury hostels in amazing locations at discount rates (I did this in Thailand and Bali and lived like a queen), there are ways you can make it work. For instance, whenever I'm staying in a hotel I'll aim to book it when it has an offer on. You can even sign up for email alerts from the hotel you've got your eye on, or phone to see when is out of season for them.

Another thing: I'm not ashamed that I like to haggle. A lot of women are scared to ask for a discount or offer, but I really do consider it the art of trading. Whether it's for a job worth £10,000 or £100, there's no harm in asking if there is wiggle room around the price. If someone says no, then that's fine – but if they can give you that little bit off, it can make your day. I have often gone back to the freelancers I have worked with over and over again because of the trust they have in me in that respect. Often that

---

1 Kayak research cited at: www.telegraph.co.uk/travel/news/cheapest-time-to-book-a-flight/

extra £10 or £100 off has meant the difference between, say, investing in more stock or hiring an additional freelancer to complete a task.

Finally, it's never too early to start saving for those big expenses that lie in the future, be that paying for your education, the rental deposit on your first flat, equipment for your side job, or hiring a graphic designer for your website – or even your retirement, crazy as that can sound. Because we will be living for longer. The typical millennial (18–34-year-olds), surveyed for Barclays, currently puts aside £200 a month or less – but a fifth save nothing at all.[1] Now, sometimes you are not in a position to save. But before you nod, 'Yes, that's me', hold on – I've got some ideas for you at the end of this chapter.

My five spending rules:

1 ALL THINGS IN GOOD TIME

First, let's acknowledge the reality: even watching the pennies, you sometimes might not have enough to do what you want; life can be expensive. For example, moving out. I stayed at home until I was twenty-six – that is now considered young in some areas. Newly married and wanting to get our first home together, Mike and I realised we would need to save more for a deposit for a home than we actually expected. That meant the dream of me being carried over the threshold was a myth for us. Mike was working at a hospital as a physiotherapist, so we ended up living in the hospital dorms because it was what we could afford. We had shared utilities, from the kitchen to the bathroom, and

---

1 newsroom.barclays.com/r/3574/old_age_pen-shunners

I remember the dash after a shower to make it back to our room without being seen by any of the doctors or nurses who lived on premises. Our room was cosy with a single bed and a sink right next to it … so chic. After around two months, I was done! Something about being cooped up in that place wasn't cute, so we moved back to my family home to continue saving and looking for that dream home. Yes, it was hell at times. As an adult, you want freedom. But we were able to save, putting together a bigger deposit for a better property and the money to transform that into a home. In total, we spent eight months at my family home. By the time we were able to move into our first place it all seemed worth it. Our new home wasn't perfect, but it was enough.

And I know I was lucky to be in a position where I could keep living at home – not everybody has that option. I did make sacrifices to get what I wanted, though. I sacrificed privacy. I certainly sacrificed glamour! And, while we're all sick of those articles that suggest millennials could have saved up for a house deposit with all the money we've spent on avocado toast and coffee (last I checked, houses were a bit more expensive than that …), most of us could save a little more if we're honest with ourselves and make it a habit. From cutting that takeaway coffee from a daily to a weekly treat, or culling a few of those 'essential' subscriptions (Netflix, Spotify, the gym), it's important to take a clear-eyed look at where your money is really going. And to do that, you need to …

2 KNOW WHAT'S GOING ON

I know, first-hand, that money – or rather a lack of it – can be a huge source of worry and anxiety. So sometimes it's tempting to put our heads in the sand, leave the bills unopened or ignore that email from the bank about overdraft charges. But you can't be a boss without tackling your finances head-on.

I check my accounts regularly, not every day but enough to know what's going on. This became even more essential as I became self-employed. I was working on multiple projects at a time, which was a good thing but meant I had various payments going out at the same time. There were times when I had hit my overdraft limit when I hadn't meant to. Simply by having an invoice or two paid late by clients made a huge difference to what I had left in the bank. If you don't keep track of your cash flow you can be left in a difficult situation. I've learned that using the right resources to help me keep an eye on what's going on in my accounts makes all the difference.

Most banks these days have their own mobile app, so you can give your account a glance when you need to. For me, setting up direct debits so that regular payments are going out of my account automatically is one tool helping me manage my money. (For the running of my business I had to find other tools, more on these later.) It was important for me to find software that was going to give me transparency over my financial situation. I am no longer in the dark or scared.

These days, there are so many clever apps that can help you stay on top of your finances in more sophisticated ways, from Moneybox (moneyboxapp.com), an app that rounds up payments you make on your card to the nearest pound, on everything from coffees to Ubers, then lets you invest the difference between the actual cost and the rounded-up cost in big companies; to Squirrel (squirrel.me), that squirrels your salary away into a bank account in your name and splits it for you into bills, salary and a weekly allowance. No more ASOS splurges that leave you penniless two weeks before payday! There are new tools arriving on the market all the time.

Getting over the money dread is about more than knowing what your bank balance is – it's about really taking control. I've seen what happens when people don't put themselves in charge of their money and everything that entails. That's a big mistake, no doubt about it. In the influencer space, I've seen a lot of people make some rookie financial errors because there was no education or genuine support to teach them how to do this. To be blunt, there are a lot of influencers who will put their hand in the pot when they get a big payment, but when the taxman knocks they're nowhere to be seen! Fundamentally, it's your responsibility to look after yourself. I've learned to keep control of my money and not be afraid of the numbers. If you are not on top of your numbers, you will be burnt. Put yourself in the driving seat of your life – it really is much more interesting that way, anyway!

3 DON'T WASTE YOUR CREDIT

I am not anti credit cards or credit in general, but what I can never get behind is not using your credit wisely. Credit makes the world go round and if you ruin your credit scores – effectively, your financial reputation – it can have a knock-on effect in the future. So don't waste it!

Don't use your credit to buy *stuff*, is my rule. What I mean is, if you're using a credit card to buy shoes, bags or clothes, that is not a way to use credit wisely – you're just accumulating more things. What's more, unless you pay off your card in full every month, you're probably getting charged extra for using the bank's money to buy all that, so it's costing you more than it needs to. And the worst thing you can do is get into a habit of buying things you can't afford, because it can come back to bite you. Likewise, I personally would never recommend buying on store cards. These are cards that you can only use in one store, often giving you a tempting introductory discount. However, recent research found two-thirds of these charge more than 25 per cent interest, which is far higher than standard credit cards.[1]

There are a few situations where it can be sensible to use a credit card, however, such as when you need to make a big purchase like a holiday, as a credit card gives you certain consumer protections that a debit card doesn't if anything goes wrong. And, if you're smart, you can use your credit to build up a financial profile for the future. For example, if you want to be approved for a mortgage to buy a house, the bank will check your credit history, while some employers may also check it before you start a job. Similarly, if you want to start a business, some potential partners will check your credit history before ever working with you.

If you do start using a credit card to build up your credit score, borrow responsibly. Buy what you need and within your grasp, set up a direct debit to pay off balances in full automatically and keep an eye on it. If you're smart you may get to a position where you are able to borrow large amounts, use that to invest in ventures, turn a profit and pay back the balance without it costing you anything. Someone once told me that smart people use other

1 MoneySavingExpert, cited in www.theguardian.com/money/2017/jul/08/debt-store-cards-sky-high-interest-rates-growing-problem-complaints

people's money to make money – and that's a key principle of investing to remember.

4 SET GOALS (THEN GET EDUCATED)

I'm giving you my need-to-know on money matters, but over and above everything else, the golden rule is to identify what's important to you. When I started taking an interest in personal finance, it's because I tuned in to what was important to me: at the time it was buying a property. That became *my* goal. Just by establishing your 'why?' something amazing happens. Because goal-setting really does make it more likely you will get what you want. One study by a psychologist, professor Gail Matthews of the Dominican University of California, found that when people wrote down their business-related goals, they were significantly more successful in achieving them compared to those who kept their goals in their head.[1] (And sharing their goal with a friend made it even more likely again that they would hit it. Time to grab a pen and start writing to your auntie about that flat with a 'For Sale' sign …)

Then, get educated in that area, so you can break down the steps involved in hitting that goal. Suddenly, something that can seem unachievable, will become more concrete simply by doing this exercise. To me, buying a house sounded incredibly daunting, and I know I'm not alone in that! But it doesn't mean you can't try. Ultimately, I realised I just had to break my goal down into steps:

> One, look at how much money I needed for a deposit.

1 https://www.dominican.edu/dominicannews/study-highlights-strategies-for-achieving-goals

> Two, save for a deposit (and that might take a very long time!).

> Three, make sure my payments – when I got a mortgage – would be affordable.

My goals have now changed and developed, but the same principle applies whatever you are aiming for: getting educated in what you want and why, then taking the steps to achieve that will make all the difference. And talk to people! Learn from others' experiences. In your case, you might be looking to getting together enough money to launch a business. How much is that going to cost you, realistically? Once you've a good understanding of what it is you're attempting to do, you start to see if it's achievable or if you're going to have to rethink your plan, or attempt to do it another way. But you're still making progress with your financial goal, rather than giving up because other people have told you it's impossible.

5 GIVE IT AWAY NOW

Don't forget to give some of your hard-earned cash away. No, I'm not joking. I'm a saver, but that doesn't mean I'm stingy. In fact, it's the opposite. When I got my first pay cheque, when I was sixteen and in a part-time job, I gave my family part of it. It's tradition in my culture – you give your parents a section of what you have, out of respect. And now I give 10 per cent of my earnings to charity; it's a discipline that I've found has made me more positive towards my finances. I genuinely believe that the more you give, the more you get (this might not be monetary but can manifest in so many forms). Studies show there's something in that: yes, you *feel* wealthier when you give, according to research from Harvard Business School.[1] But it's more than that. Not only do people give more when they're richer – that makes sense – but it seems to work the other way too: researchers have found that people also tend to grow wealthier when they give more.[2] It seems thinking charitably helps us be more successful.

Some people have said to me that sometimes I can be a bit overgenerous. If someone tells me, 'I need money', I'll say, 'That's alright, I'll give it to you' – and I never expect to get it back. If you do and someone lets you down, you'll be upset and angry – and that's negative energy that you don't need in your life. I always give what I know I can afford to lose, so I won't be left out of pocket if I don't get it back. That's definitely happened, but it's not something I've dwelled on.

Five steps to five k

I want to go another step further. As I said, I like concrete measurable goals, so you know when you've hit them – and can move on to the next one. It's motivating. So I'm challenging you to save up a particular amount: £5K! Why? It's a significant yet achievable amount that's going to focus your attention and energy. It's hugely helpful in covering the costs of starting up a business or getting a new venture off the ground if you're thinking you want to go it alone. In fact, while figures vary, a report by The Company Warehouse, a business services website, found that £5,000 is

---

1 www.acrwebsite.org/volumes/16264/volumes/v38/NA-38
2 www.aei.org/publication/giving-makes-you-rich/

actually the average budget for start-up businesses in the UK.[1] And, when you've hit that target, you'll have a real chunk of money that you can use as a foundation for a lot of different things.

Start-up costs will be different for every business, but with that sum you can buy a domain name, create a website, get your IT equipment and much more. Perhaps you're planning to do business over a website and app? That could be £450 (and counting) for a lawyer to nail down your terms and conditions, thank you. Ready to make your first hire? Another £250, minimum, to get an employment agreement sorted and do it all by the book.[2] Then you'll want an accountant to check you're not going to run into a tax headache like I did ... more on that in a bit. An accountant can easily start at £300 or more. Costs are higher than expected for one in three new business owners, and younger entrepreneurs, 18- to 34-year-olds, are more likely to be taken by surprise by those costs than older start-up owners, according to a survey by Lloyds Bank – and no wonder.

So, save yourself the headache and get a generous buffer of money so you don't end up maxing out your overdraft when unexpected costs arise (and there are *always* unexpected costs). Here's how you're going to do it ...

1   SAVE YOURSELF

I've already explained how my experiences have prompted me to be a saver rather than a splurger – I spend what I need to spend, and everything else goes in the bank until I'm ready to make a

---

1 www.thecompanywarehouse.co.uk/blog/what-is-the-average-startup-budget
2   www.lexoo.co.uk/legal-price-index

move and put it to good use. But there's no point saving your cash unless you're putting it somewhere you're not going to touch it. Don't let it slosh about in the current account you use every day – keep it separate. I like to have multiple different accounts, for my personal and business needs. Different banks will offer different deals on their savings accounts at different times, so check the interest rates – how much money *your* money can earn while it's in the bank. Or, you might try an ISA, which is basically a tax-free savings account. You can find up-to-date information online. The more you save, the more motivated you will be to find the best account to maximise your savings.

2   TURN YOUR TRASH INTO TREASURE

It's true: one woman's trash is another woman's treasure. Which means you can make money by selling the stuff you don't need, don't want, and that isn't adding to your life. Be brutal as you go through your wardrobe and your possessions to see what you no longer use or need, but which someone else might. Use your head here, not your heart. You might feel sentimentally attached to an item when you don't need to be. Then, list it all on eBay or rival clothes-selling website Depop, which I've started using. Yes, even now, I sell clothes that I don't wear any more, and I know I'm not the only person in my field who does. (If you're really pressed for time, you can even use a site like returntoearn.co.uk, which will pick up a bag of clothes and value it for you, based on weight.) Be ruthless. What will find a new lease of life in someone else's wardrobe?

3 YOUR TIME REALLY IS MONEY

In my main line of work as a YouTuber I am not selling something tangible – I'm lucky enough to be in the position where people are interested in what I am saying, thinking and sharing. So remember, you don't have to have a product to sell. You will have a skill, gift or ability that you can monetise in some way. Come up with one thing that you're good at doing, that you enjoy doing, and then offer it locally or globally – or both. Does this sound familiar? I hope so, because the same questions you asked your-self about finding your grind as an influencer are relevant here. If you're playing to your strengths, the areas you're thinking about should overlap or even be one and the same. That way, even as you're getting together money for whatever's your grand plan, you can be honing your skills, earning endorsements and feedback from clients, and finding out if this gig will really work for you on a bigger scale.

One of my friends makes wigs, for instance. Rather than just sell them, she set up a class where people pay hundreds of pounds to learn from her how to make wigs. She's not giving away her products to those people paying her; she's giving away her knowl-edge. Instantly, she has added another strand to her business – she's no longer limited by how long it might take her to handmake a single wig. She can provide a service to multiple people at a time, leveraging those same skills. And, niche as it may sound, she has found an audience: people who fly in from around the world to do her classes. I work with a girl who loves graphic design and offers her services on a retainer model, so she has regular clients – including me – who pay her to work for them regularly: she works on everything from web design, to helping to curate

Instagram feeds, to helping with fonts, colours and a consistent look of a brand. She found me on Twitter, as she does all her clients, and offers her skills to people all over the world. You can still do old-school marketing too: knock on doors in your area to tell people what you're up to; print business cards and flyers and put them through letterboxes. There's always a way to earn.

4 CAN YOU DO MORE?

The best of us have times when we need to multiply our income streams. Which is a fancy way of saying, get an extra job. There is nothing wrong with working overtime for someone else as a way to put yourself in the best position to eventually be your own boss. All things in good time! No one wants to be working round the clock, but sometimes you just need to get your head down and grind. Again, here I turn for inspiration to my mum: one time, she was buying products here to sell them in Nigeria, her own side hustle; but she also had her job cleaning offices and, on top of that, she'd clean trains. (Yes, and she was also training to be a nurse.) Somehow, she made it work. You don't have to have just one job. Even if you've a nine to five in the week, you could pick up bar work on a Saturday night, so you can do something sociable and earn some extra money that you can put towards your £5K target and help you get to where you really want to be.

5 TURN TRADER

At the very simplest level, buying something and selling it for a bit more is the most straightforward way to make money. The Internet is a great way to source exciting products that you think you could sell locally. Or, conversely, you could offer items that are only available locally to the whole world! That's what all those arty types on Etsy are doing, selling the handcrafted items they are making at home all around the globe. Once you've stocked up, you could have a sale aimed at friends and family, at first; later, a broader community, or sell your product online. In fact, I do that myself … as I'll explain in a moment.

But what can *you* sell? Again, I want you to think about that intersection of passion, ability and audience (explained in chapter one) – in this case, tweaked to passion, knowledge and market. Ask yourself these three questions:

> What do I like?

> What do I know about?

> What might people want to buy from me?

I want to share with you what I've discovered:

NICHE WORKS: So long as your product finds some fans, it's fine if it's not to everyone's taste. I know a girl who has a side business in selling sex toys – blow-up dolls. Now, that's really niche! I'm not sure how she got into it and I won't be asking. But there's a market for it. It's simply monetary: the mark-up she can put on the dolls she buys is big, and it's not a saturated market. OK, that may not be for you! But she saw an opportunity and went for it. What I don't recommend is getting wrapped up in the product. It's better to be wrapped up in what you can afford.

BUY CHEAP: You've got to make sure you can buy your product at a price that allows you to sell it on at a profit, compensating you for the time and costs involved. By hunting out bargains you will find items you can easily sell at a comfortable mark-up. On sites such as eBay and Alibaba you can source suppliers from all over the world, selling products at big discounts to what you'd find in the shops. I know people can be scared to buy direct from these companies: business is often about being willing to take the risk that others won't. And you might lose your money if you buy from an unfamiliar supplier that you haven't checked out. Or, your risk might lie in putting in a bulk order that means you get a discount; you need to be confident you can shift that amount of product.

START SMALL: Tread carefully, to manage that risk. First, test it – don't spend all your money, but rather try to get a sample for free, if possible. Just ask the vendor. If the sample impresses you, put in a small order. Test it: are you happy with the quality? Would you spend your own money on it, if you were in your customer's shoes. Is there demand for it? Then, and only then, think about scaling up. Don't just spend all your money in one go.

ADD VALUE: Selling online isn't the only model, of course. I know people who buy their product on eBay, then sell it in person, at car boot sales, for example, to people who don't want to trawl through pages online. Or, they might sell through their own website, making the most of their own strong personal taste to offer a great, curated selection of items online. The fundamental idea remains the same: you are adding value, be that speed, ease, or quality. For instance, I used to buy job lots of buttons and trims on eBay from old haberdasheries getting rid of stock. Some of what would turn up in the post would be great, some would not. I would use the items I liked to customise clothes – but, equally, if I had decided to go through that stock, and curate the attractive items, perhaps presenting a set of ten gold vintage-style buttons on a card, I would have added value. Curation is worth something.

How I made money by adding value

You might be asking: But can I really do this, Patricia? Yes, you definitely can – because I have. If I can, you can too. YouTube is my focus these days, but I am all about exploring other options to keep things interesting: these five steps are all actions that I have taken – and, in fact, continue to take – in my everyday life. These days, as well as dealing with my social channels, I also work really hard on my company Y-HAIR, which sells beautiful hair extensions. And it all came about because I spotted a niche in the market – prompted by my own needs.

It was around 2010 when my friend and I were googling Beyoncé's hair – she seemed to be wearing a really great, natural-looking hair-piece, and we wondered what it was. After searching online we discovered it was what's called a lace-front wig. The beauty of this type of hairpiece is that they give you a really natural-looking hairline, but they were hard to get hold of. I got stuck into finding a manu-facturer, to source these products for myself. This process was very hit-and-miss, and I was scammed a number of times, but eventually I was able to find a supplier who again and again provided excellent extensions. Over time we developed a working relationship and I knew I could trust him to supply quality products. So, when people started to ask me about my hairpieces and extensions, I thought: *I've a supplier I trust, I'm already importing hair for my own needs as good-quality hair is hard to come by – so why don't I just scale this up?* And so Y-HAIR was born!

I didn't brand the hair company after myself, as I wanted to focus on the customer, not me. So it's Y-HAIR – associated with 'yeah hair' and 'why (y) not'? (People get caught up in naming their business, but it really doesn't matter as much as your product and service. A name is easy to change.) With Y-HAIR, we deliver a high-quality product, supported by a rapid delivery service and an easy returns process. That's how we add value to the stock we import.

Back at the start, I invested £8,000 to buy the stock and get it to the UK. So I used the majority of my savings at the time. I had to get over the fear of losing that money to start something – and that was far from the only outlay. I had to pay for shoots to display the products, I had to buy my packaging, I had to pay my logistics company, which would handle distribution. I'd realised I didn't have time to handle orders, so, after visiting trade shows to find suitable partners, I found a company with the warehouse staff to do so. It took six to seven months to get my initial investment back.

Once you're up and running, the challenges are different. You have to make sure your customer is happy – and learn how to handle any queries or concerns. I've faced my share of would-be scammers: people saying they've been charged for an order that hadn't arrived, when they hadn't even placed one with us! Still, I knew that we always had to respond respectfully. Anyone can screenshot an email and tell a story that makes you look bad, even if it's not true – so you have to be careful. Always behave as if the customer's always right – even when they're not really your customer!

LIFE LESSON: Now that my hair business is up and running it puts fewer demands on my time. Getting a venture off the ground is the hardest aspect of starting something. Once you've got the momentum, you're good. So what's stopping you?

YOUR ACTION PLAN

You've got my list of ideas for getting together £5,000 that will help you make your dreams a reality. Whatever your saving goal is, or whatever stage it's at, I want you to write it down here. It doesn't matter if your grand plan changes over time or if you're scarce on detail. Write down 'going freelance' or 'running my own business' or 'leaving my day job at last!' It's helpful to have an idea in mind other than just 'saving':

YOUR SAVING GOAL:

Now, get a cup of tea or whatever you like to drink and have another think. How might you start to save your first £5K towards that goal?

YOUR FIVE STEPS TO FIVE K:

1. First things first. Where are you going to keep all this lovely money? A savings account / ISA / stick it under the mattress with the rest of your valuables (please don't do this)? Identify where you can keep these funds separate from the cash you access day-to-day.

2. Time to toss out the trash and make some cash. What do you own that you no longer wear, use or want? And where could you sell it?

3. You've already been thinking about your grind. Now, consider how you can monetise it – even if you're still getting it off the ground. If you're all about music and want to have your own record label, could you be offering singing lessons online or recording jingles for local businesses? If you want to make a living from your art and launch an online gallery, could you paint portraits for friends and family? Be sure to put what you do and know out there (social media is a great place to start).

4. What products do you love or know a lot about? Is there anything you could source and sell to friends and family, or even locally and online?

5. Could you work an extra job at the weekends or in the evenings, or pick up more shifts at work, to earn a bit of money to get your project off the ground? Be honest with yourself – we're all busy, but most of us tend to spend a few more hours phone-scrolling in front of Netflix than we'd like to admit.

8 | A career vs going it alone

So far, I've talked a lot about running your own business, since some of us want to make our hustle a fully-fledged career. For others, your side-hustle might be just a stepping stone in a much bigger plan, providing you with the knowledge and experience needed to make the next move. Whatever side of the fence you sit on (and there's nothing wrong with trying both!), I learned some valuable lessons on my personal journey towards 'going it alone', which I'm going to share in this next section …

Making my voice heard

Flashback to my City girl days. On my first day in the office after joining the bank as a graduate trainee, I remember being very concerned about what my suit looked like. And I didn't see anyone I knew. As an intern, it had felt more like a community; when you're a graduate, you all go off to your separate areas. I sat in a row of six or so desks, near our manager's office, and we didn't really interact with the other rows near us. I was the youngest on the team and one of very few women when I started in that department, 'Prime Brokerage Technology' – I didn't even really know what that meant!

I don't mind saying that I went through a period where I thought, *I can't do this*. I was very quiet, very shy, like a little dormouse. A lot of people wouldn't believe it now! But I got feedback saying: 'You need to speak up more, you need to be involved.' At the time I was worried: I felt I'd be talking rubbish and just be in the way if I kept asking loads of questions. My attitude was, *I'll just sit here quietly*. The problem with that approach is that if you're not saying anything, if you're not talking about work, or asking for more work – you may end up not doing much! I started to realise that they were giving me mediocre tasks, like creating folders in a shared drive for the team – dogsbody work. I can only say this in hindsight; all I knew at the time was that I just felt very much out of the loop, like I didn't fit in.

About five months into my time there, a contractor joined the team. She was much older than me, in her forties, and was just a force to be reckoned with. She was way more senior than me, but I couldn't believe how quickly she'd gone in, learned what to do, and taken responsibility. I thought to myself, *Man, I've got to be more like that*. She was such a strong, boisterous personality – and, most importantly, she knew what she was talking about. I realised that you can't just sit quietly or take a guess at what's going on. I needed to better learn to ask questions and really understand.

Years passed, and I was feeling a lot more settled. The things I'd been unsure about, I had begun to work through. I felt especially supported by a number of different mentors, specifically some of the women I worked with. I really learned to become a researcher, teach myself what I didn't know, be louder, ask questions and speak up. It took a while, but when I got there it was worth it.

Should I try to fit in?

We can limit ourselves if we assume that we can't work with other people who are different to us. Being a black woman in a very male, mostly white environment, I didn't necessarily blend in. But you're always going to come across people who are different to you in life – sometimes you're going to need to find a way to connect, and it needs to happen both ways. On my team, the guys were into running, talking about their best times, and discussing their 'primal' diet. What the hell that was, I didn't know! But I acted as if I cared, say, 'That's really interesting, tell me more about that.' I'd pretend I knew what was going on, then do some research on the weekend, and when the opportunity to talk about what they'd been discussing came up again I would drop in the little knowledge I had, to be a bit more included in the conversation. 'I saw that thing about the primal diet,' I might say. 'It looks quite good, I might try it.' Now, I didn't – you're supposed to eat like a caveman and eliminate all processed foods! – but there's nothing wrong with making an effort to join in.

I've never been a pub girl, never a drinker, but the work culture was that everyone would have a drink together at the end of the week, so I'd go along. And I kept myself open to making new connections. Make a bit of an effort, and you'll find people who you really get on with.

• •

LIFE LESSON: You can connect with almost anybody based on how willing you are to be open to them. Some people don't want to be open to you and that's fine – don't worry about them – but sometimes it really is about the way that *you* are willing to relate to other people.

• •

Facing the axe

It can happen to the best of us, and I was made redundant at the bank after two and half years, during a bad time for the markets. I learned you can lose your job for reasons totally out of your control. That was scary – I'd always had the security of having an internship or graduate programme until that moment. I dusted myself off and got in touch with loads of headhunters, who started to call me about jobs they had on their books.

Eventually, I ended up working as a consultant for Deloitte, a big company with a good reputation. As much as I'd thought banking was hard, consulting was harder. My role was to be the bridging person between a company's business and technology processes – I would tell companies how they should integrate the two. With clients to report to, I worked hard, from seven in the morning to midnight. I would finish a report and hand it to a director at 8 p.m., and it would come back to me with changes I needed to hand back at 10 p.m. The environment was competitive, and putting in face time in the office was important. I was newly married and the hours were a shock to both me and Mike.

But, hard as I worked, I thrived, because I learned so much. If I had a project, it was my project. I was in control of something. And I learned to give as good as I got – I had to. I remember sitting at a table, when I was acting as the lead consultant on a project, faced with our client, a chief executive. I was telling him what I thought he should be doing to improve processes at his organisation. He was just giving me this look that said, *But why?* I knew he was annoyed because the senior consultant wasn't there and it was only him and me. I just had to hold my ground, and share my knowledge. Slowly but surely, he could see that I knew what I was talking about, that I really did have something to offer, and wasn't there to waste either his or my time. By the end of the meeting, we were getting on fine.

Eventually I thought, *I don't want to do this long term*. I'm not a quitter, but once I'm done, I'm done. But I learned so much about business in that role. Today, when I come up with ideas and work with my own team, I'm using so many of the skills I developed there.

• •

LIFE LESSON: Being made redundant may be the best thing that could happen to you. It was for me. At the time it didn't feel like it, but actually it's been an upward trajectory since then.

• •

The manager who made me cry

I want to share something else with you: I had a really bad manager early on in my career. I won't name him or the office. Even now, I hate thinking about it. He was just really harsh. I was young, under-confident, and he made me feel so stupid, asking questions like, 'Why would you do that?', 'So what makes you think that should go there?' and 'I thought you did accounting?', and he would shout at me in front of everybody, making it extra awkward. I couldn't believe how horrible he was. Eventually, we were in a meeting together and I started crying while he was talking to me. He didn't even realise that what he was saying was upsetting me until I began bawling. Finally, he apologised and I had to mop up my tears in the bathroom.

The one thing I'll give him is that he was quite snappy with everyone – it wasn't a personality clash with me in particular. And, I'll be honest with you, I had a lot to learn at that stage of my career – but he wasn't good at teaching me how to be better. He could have delivered his criticism in a way that didn't feel so personal. After the meeting where I cried, I noticed he was a bit nicer to me. I think he just hadn't realised how much what he was saying was getting to me. He still wasn't the ideal boss, but he was calmer and made more effort to explain things as I'd asked him to do.

How to handle a boss from hell

Unfortunately, most of us will go through something similar: the average worker is saddled with two bad bosses in a lifetime.[1] My

---

1 www.telegraph.co.uk/finance/jobs/11975788/Britons-in-the-workplace-The-figures-that-lay-bare-the-life-of-an-average-British-employee.html

advice if you've got a boss who makes you dread going into work is this: 1) remember it happens to the best of us! 2) find someone you can share the issue with: another member of management or a team member, to discuss a constructive approach – or, if you're confident enough, talk to your boss. That way, you're addressing the issue head on.

It's important to be clear about what is it that you don't like. What I didn't like about my situation was that this guy was very critical of what I was doing, but he wasn't showing me how to do it better. When we had a training session together, it felt like it was more of an opportunity for him to say, 'You're doing it wrong. Why don't you know this?' rather than help me get to grips with my work. Try to explain to the person how the situation is affecting you and, as far as you can, what you would prefer to happen, so you can address the problems.

At the same time, if it's a performance issue – try to get better! You might feel like giving up, but you've got to put the work in. I was not a perfect employee, and my boss was getting frustrated. If none of this is improving the situation, you could ask for someone else to report into, if that seems like an option. And if you've exhausted all your options, and the situation is not improving? Then jog on! Look for another job.

In time, I flourished. If I do say it myself, I was a great employee! I had doubted myself, and it didn't help at all. Later in my career, I encountered other tricky people at work, but I had a thicker skin and was more secure in my abilities – that had come through experience – so it just didn't ruffle me so much.

• •

LIFE LESSON: Some situations can't be saved –
and if you've tried everything, and the situation's
unbearable, start planning your escape. You don't
want to be in an environment where you don't feel
respected, because it means you're never going to
be the best employee you could possibly be.

• •

Above all, keep your eye on the prize. Remember: every job
you have is a stepping stone, not the finishing post. Once you've
settled into your current role, and you've got some reliable cash
coming in, it's time to focus on building your personal brand, as
I've already explained. That will put you in the best possible
position to pursue what you *really* want to do when you get that
itch and feel it might be time to make a move.

In my case, that was for me to make my move as a YouTuber.
In yours, it might be something completely different: going freelance, setting up your own business, or perhaps some other project
that I've not yet even imagined! But many of us will reach the
point when it's time to step away from the safety of the office
cubicle or another daily routine and go full-steam ahead with
what's really important to us.

So, how do you know when it's time for you to …

Decide to jump?

The first thing to say, is that if you're trying to do everything, you're never going to be able to give anything quality time. It's important to focus on two, maybe three maximum, opportunities at one time. For more than four years, that's what I did: out front, everything looked great, I was building my career, but every weekend I would work on my social media. I'd say I spent roughly 80 per cent of my energy working in a full-time role, and 20 per cent on my YouTube. And, in fact, there's something called the 80:20 rule, a business theory that 20 per cent of your efforts will generate 80 per cent of your results, however you want to classify them – earnings, say. And that's what eventually happened for me.

I had around 100,000 subscribers to my channel and I was building traction online. It got to the stage when I couldn't go and do projects to do with my channel – a shoot, for example – because I was working at the day job. I could only do things at the weekends. That's the moment – when it's getting to the point where your side hustle is being held back by your main job – when you know that you should think about taking the leap.

All right, I thought, *It's time for the switchover.*

Reaching for a life raft

But it wasn't that simple. Leaving the world of employment was a nerve-wracking and scary process. What actually happened is that I left my job and said, 'I'm going to be a full-time YouTuber!' Then I panicked. Let me explain …

At the time, I'd moved on from my consulting job, after being headhunted to work in business analysis at the Bank of Tokyo. They'd offered me a good salary: £50,000 and another £10,000 on top of that, for signing on with them. It was the best job I could have hoped for: great people, excellent money, and with an amazing work/life balance. But there was always this little voice inside me, saying. 'Patricia, you should do YouTube.' I remember sitting at my desk and thinking, can I balance the two? Or do I want to quit and do YouTube full time? I'd taken some days off to shoot with brands, getting some early sponsorships for my channel, but it just wasn't practical to put my all into chasing two goals at once: my corporate career and my own business.

Take calculated risks

So I opened up an Excel spreadsheet – because that's the kind of person I am! – and started doing my sums. What would it look like if I had more sponsorship offers for my channel, perhaps one a month, or two or three times a month, over, say, five years? Then I made a calculation as to how much I thought my salary would grow over the same five years, taking into account inflation and possible promotions. The result shocked me: quitting my job could be a better option for me financially if I really focused on growing my YouTube channel. What I loved doing could actually be more lucrative! I hadn't worked at the bank for more than a few months when I left to work on my own project – again.

I was very clear-headed: by that point Mike and I were settled in our home and we had some savings in the bank. He had a job and our mortgage payments were low, so we had enough money to live on. I was comfortable enough (or so I thought) to make the leap. I had potential and a plan.

• •

LIFE LESSON: When you're planning a major change, define what it is that's important to you. For me, it was having some form of security. I stayed in a traditional workplace until I was a homeowner. Then, I knew I could afford food, my mortgage and maybe one holiday a year. That was my baseline and everything else represented a level of risk I could handle.

• •

Getting cold feet

Great, I thought, *I'm going to be a boss, a full-time YouTuber.* The reality was … different. My husband would go off to work, and I would be sitting at home, not quite knowing what to do, not really making as many videos as I'd thought I would, and all the while a nasty little thought was running through my mind: *Uh-oh. Maybe I shouldn't have done this.* One morning, I remember thinking, *How am I still in bed at 11.30? Normally, I'm on the train by 7.00. Gosh, there's no one to tell me what to do.* I wasn't quite ready for that. I liked the routine of wake up in the morning, get dressed, go to work, come back. I told myself, *I can't do this, I don't know what I'm going to do, I'm going to fail, I'm not going to make enough money.* I panicked – after no more than three weeks.

So I contacted someone I knew in the social media world and told him, 'I quit my job.' My channel used to be connected to what's called a multi-channel network (MCN) called Base79. Its co-creator, who I would consider a mentor, said to me, 'Come and work for us if you want to.' I ended up working there, four days a week, so I had time to spend on my own stuff. Again, the job looked perfect. Now I was consulting for brands on YouTube videos and giving advice to companies on building their social profiles. I didn't feel like I'd given up on a dream; I felt maybe I'd found an alternative career that would make me happy.

But do you know what? Until then, I didn't really know the potential of my own business. However, working inside a social media-based company and dealing with big brands gave me a little bit more insight into the potential of my channel. I thought, *Hold on. The opportunity's bigger than I thought it was going to be. I can do this.* There was a shift in my mindset: I could now see the path ahead more clearly. Finally, I'd reached my real tipping point. I was ready to jump.

So I did that job for three months, then I left to do YouTube full time. I don't feel bad about taking my time to make the leap. Mike Lewis, author of *When to Jump*, about people switching careers to go for their dreams, calls it 'the 10,000 un-sexy steps' you take before you make that big change.

• •

LIFE LESSON: While it may feel like you're taking one step forwards and one step backwards, you can't expect to just move along in a straight line. I don't have any regrets.

• •

Push through the fear

I want to share something that's particularly important when you're thinking of taking the leap into a new stage of your life. When we're struggling or fearful about something we want to do, the temptation is to reach for an excuse. Don't. Excuses are just ways to stop yourself from being as good as you want to be. Ditch them!

For instance, starting out in business, you might tell yourself, *I'm too young to do this.* No, you're not. Equally, I know so many older women – in the social media space, in particular – who are amazing at what they do and extremely well respected. They bring their wisdom to the table, while other people bring their youth. It's all valuable. 'Too young' or 'too old' – they're just excuses. I'm black – that could be an excuse. I'm a mum too, I've got a mortgage to pay. And, if you looked at where I've come from, I probably had everything stacked against me.

But I'm just not going to let anything limit me. Instead, I see all my qualities as assets. Don't let anything about yourself be an excuse for not going as far as you could.

TURN YOUR EXCUSES
INTO ASSETS

I want you to write down all the things that you worry about – that you think could hold you back. Then, in the column next to each one, I want you to think of a reason why that thing could actually help you. If you're broke, could that make you hungry to succeed? If you come from a background that isn't the mainstream, does that mean you have valuable insights into an audience or a group of customers that are being ignored? Write them down. Turn your pros into cons.

9 | How to run your empire

Now you're in at the deep end, and the truth is, success brings its own challenges. It's great to have them – these are the problems you want to face as an entrepreneur – but you've got to tackle them. And whatever stage you're at, you can start to get on top of these now rather than later.

Be a queen of the list

Now, I wouldn't say that I know how to run my business and my life perfectly. A lot of the time, I am pulling my hair out! Nonetheless, I have ways of trying to deal with it. I'm queen of the list, and I am queen of scheduling. I'm obsessed with writing things down because if it's all in my head everything gets jumbled up and can be very overwhelming. I work with a year-to-view calendar, so I can literally see what I've got coming up.

And I plan. You already know I am Excel obsessive – I live for it. Coming from the financial world, I used to use a lot of tables, and data was always coming in and out of Excel spreadsheets.

Right now, the data I'm managing might be not always be numerical, but it still needs to be managed in a way that's easy for me to process. So I use spreadsheets and I have different columns to list the things I need to do for each of my responsibilities: Instagram, YouTube, Facebook, Twitter, potential business opportunities, even to-do items for my personal life. I know not everyone uses spreadsheets, but you can use a diary, Google Docs, online project management tool Asana or even a piece of paper that you divide into sections – experiment to find what suits you.

Don't deal with more than today

I try not to look at everything at once. Because if you're looking way too far ahead, you can start to feel a bit daunted. What I will do is sit down on a Sunday night, or at the latest, Monday morning, and pick items from each area of my list – Instagram, YouTube, my personal life and so on – and decide that I will deal with those items in the coming week. Then I'll break it down by day too, working on a piece of paper or my actual diary to divvy up my tasks day by day.

Crucially, I try not to put too much on my daily list. Sometimes, I'll have only five tasks to do in a day, and if I can cross off half of those, I'll be happy. For instance, as I write today, I know I've also got to get some videos edited. I also have Instagram pictures that I want to edit and prepare to post, but I plan to do them later in the week so that I don't have to think about that right now. Later, in the evening, I'll check: what did I achieve today? Did I get it all done? And then, if I need to, I'll update my list of things that I aim to do the next day.

But I make sure not to overload myself: if you have forty things on your to-do list, there are just not enough hours in the day to get through them, so your organisational tool becomes just another source of stress.

● ●

LIFE LESSON: I feel that for people who are creative or self-employed, there isn't an off switch – our minds are always going. For me to relax, I have to actively write down the things I need to do. Get it out of your head and onto paper, so your brain knows, *OK, downtime now.*

● ●

Train as a (time)boxer

I often timebox – set out an hour-by-hour plan of my day. So, my afternoon might look like: 1 p.m. to 2 p.m., do my makeup. Between 2 p.m. and 4 p.m., film this video. Between 4 p.m. and 5 p.m., catch up on my emails. I give myself an estimate of how long something is going to take, because it's so easy to underestimate. By the time you've done an hour-by-hour plan, you say to yourself, 'I don't have 10 minutes to waste on Instagram!' It's a great cure for procrastination. I'm fairly relaxed about how I do this: I put a lot of my commitments into Google Calendar – I use all sorts of different colours so that I can see at a glance what I'm up to. My personal time is yellow! Or I might timebox the day ahead of me on paper.

My working week

What I attempt to do is to ensure that I put aside enough time for the things that are going to develop my main product – my organic content. Otherwise, you can get pulled every which way. 'Come here, do this, go there, come to this meeting' – that's great, but it can all be a distraction from what I need to do. The beginning of the week is for me to work on YouTube videos and work on my own business projects, spending time in thought or action. On a Monday to Tuesday, I might go into my office – my team work from a co-working space in south London, where I join them if I don't want to work from home. This job is so absorbing that if I'm not careful I can get sucked in and not go anywhere! Maybe I'll go out to the gym or do errands, but otherwise I'd just be here on my laptop, which also isn't healthy. Or I might film videos all day; and I might spend some time sitting down and editing them with my editor remotely. As the week progresses, I'll be out and about more: Thursdays and Fridays tend to be when I'll go out to events, meetings, and get some creative input.

LIFE LESSON: When you work from home, you can dress however you want – in theory. I could sit in my pyjamas all day, every day, but it doesn't make me feel great. When I put my makeup on and brush my hair, I feel a bit more ready to face the day. Get dressed and fit for the day – you don't have to be doing the full Kim Kardashian all the time, but make an effort for yourself.

Growing pains

When your business starts to grow, you will need to hire people to work with you, whether that's full time, part time or on a freelance basis. I find that so much of the growth I've enjoyed is because I've had the people around me who helped me grow. I look for those who work hard, bring something to the table and who use their own initiative. Personally, I am really open to giving people a chance. Not only does it mean that you create links with people you wouldn't necessarily have considered who can make a positive impact on your business, but as the hirer, you gain an insight into how to impress potential employers you're super keen to work for but who might not be advertising any positions, or even know they need you (yet!). In other words, the dreaded networking ...

Embrace the new networking

People hear 'networking' and think it means going to drinks parties where they don't know anyone. Uh, no, that's so awful! Networking is subtle, real and genuine. For me, it's as simple as commenting on your favourite person's feed, sending the odd friendly DM and being receptive to what's going on in people's lives. People are sharing everything online, so if there's something in someone's life that you connect with – perhaps you like the same kind of dog, or you eat the same breakfast – notice these little cues that people are giving out about what interests them. It makes it very easy to find common ground with someone – and then you've opened up a conversation.

I've connected with people who have, literally, 100 followers and others who've got a million followers. It just has to be genuine and without expectation. People can be quite sceptical: it may look like someone is only wanting to connect with you because you've got something they want, be that followers, influence or anything else. So if you're the person reaching out, what you want to do is bring something valuable to the table, too, so it's not a one-way relationship. Eventually something might come of it – and great! – but that should never be the assumption.

How do you do that? Here's an example of what works. A few years ago, a girl called Alice messaged me on Facebook to offer her services for free: 'Can I come in and spend some time working with you?' She started working with me editing my photos, and then one thing led to another. She didn't know how to use Final Cut Pro, the video-editing software I mentioned earlier that I edit with nowadays, but we learned how to do that together. She did such great work that after a month I gave her a permanent job and she stayed with me for three years after graduating, before moving on to work at a great shoe brand as their head photographer and videographer. That's the way I like to build connections – with people who have something to offer, something going on.

Funnily enough, this is a great principle to apply to your personal life, too. For instance, some people I meet in my world only want to talk about social media. Yes, it's great to be engaged with your work, but you want to be a well-rounded person. Sometimes, I think to myself, *It'd be great if I were fencing on the weekend or cooking vegan recipes. Anything but more social media chat!* If you have something interesting going on, you can share that with others, and vice versa. That's how you build any relationship.

· ·

LIFE LESSON: Networking is not about being the best schmoozer at a cocktail party. It's about making a genuine connection and having something to offer.

· ·

And what not to do

I've had total strangers get in touch with me who just wanted to know, 'How much money do you make on YouTube' or 'Can I see your accounts?' Excuse me, are you mad?!

But there's another type of message, which seems less

problematic on the surface and which I get all the time: 'I'm starting this clothing line [or it could be a line of products or some kind of service]. I really need your help.' So, I'll have a little google, and find … nothing. There are no clothes available yet, there's no website, there's not even a holding page saying, 'Watch this space'. They've not done any of the work, yet they want me to give them my time. That's mistake number one: there's no point reaching out to people until you've got something to show them. If I saw a new clothing line and loved it, I might feature it in an Instagram post or even a video. But with these people there's nothing for me to even look at, let alone support.

The key thing, if you are reaching out to someone in a speculative way, is to have quality content, a quality product or a quality service to show them – and *evidence* of this. That may mean you have to build a portfolio of work, by doing jobs for not as much money as you would have liked, or even for free, to build a reputation. It's really not a bad idea. If you're starting out, giving someone a discount or offering a bargain, and then what you provide is really great, you're going to blow them away – and they're likely going to ask you to work for them again. It's simple, but you'd be surprised how many people don't do this!

On one occasion, I asked someone to write me a proposal for some work, and we had got to the stage of discussing costs: in the region of £100 for a day's work. In the end, I opted not to go ahead with that project and messaged the person to say, 'Thank you so much. Please send me an invoice for the proposal' – me assuming it would be £200 or £300, for a couple of days' work. They invoiced me for £1,700! Now, that was definitely not what I was expecting on the basis of the proposal I'd been sent. I was flabbergasted, especially because I knew this person relatively well. That left a sour taste. I thought, Yep, sure I'll pay you that, but I will never ask you to do anything for me again. They had tried to rip me off and yes, got their money, but in the long term they lost out, because there is no chance of any other work coming their way from me, or of me recommending that person to anyone else.

Avoid the common pitfalls

Along the way, I've noticed that people can make certain mistakes when they try to go it alone – whether that's pursuing a side project or focusing on their business full time. I made a lot of them! Here are a few to avoid …

1   TALK IS EXPENSIVE

It's great to promote yourself: tweet about what you're doing, encourage your friends and family to spread the word about your venture. However, some people want everybody to know they're an entrepreneur. And that's it! They're more caught up with the idea of running their own business than the nitty-gritty. Ignoring the numbers is a huge mistake. Yes, business is about doing something that you like, but if you're making a loss every month, then it's not yet a business – just a pain in the ass! Sometimes it's important to be quiet and hustle, getting your head down and putting in the work rather than just talking about it.

2   STAY ON TOP OF YOUR NUMBERS

So you're making money. Well done! You also need to be keeping records. When I started to earn money from YouTube, lots of payments were going in and out of bank accounts, but I wasn't looking at my finances on a weekly or even monthly basis. As a company owner, you should check your bank account every day, or at least once a week, and schedule in that time. These days, I use Xero, a great piece of accounting software. It's an easy way to track everything that comes into my bank accounts and everything that I owe. However you want to keep track of the numbers, the most important thing is to get to grips with them early on.

3   NO NEED FOR A NASTY SURPRISE

Following on from that is the importance of staying on top of tax. I've been burnt here. While working full time in the City and making some money on the side, I went close to three years without ever properly tracking what I made or how I spent it. At some point, I realised, *I'm making money, I probably need to do something about this*, and started asking around as to what I should do. Everyone said I should get an accountant to help, so I sent my bank statements to an accounting company, who told me, 'This is what you owe for tax – and also you're late paying it, so you owe fees for that.' And I'm someone who's worked in finance! You have to educate yourself. The bottom line: if you are self-employed, you're going to have to pay your taxes yourself. There is no one, like a HR department, to hold your hand through it all. The preparation of financial statements can be a bit daunting, however there are a number of online tools that can help you, along with accountants. If you are just starting out, I suggest setting aside at least 20 per cent of your revenue to ensure you are able to pay your yearly tax bill – early!

Another shock I received was my 'VAT liability charge'. Who knew that was also a thing? Basically, once you start making money they want even more! At the time, the regulation required that anyone who turned over more than £85,000 per year charged this tax to the client and then paid it back to the government. That meant that with each customer invoice I was supposed to add an additional 20 per cent to what I was charging them. It was almost two years before I realised that I had met this VAT threshold twice over, and more. But I had not charged my clients anything, so I was liable for a huge VAT bill, and due a fine (I've had to pay a number of these, back in the day!). I went through the painstaking exercise of trying to ask past clients to pay up more money two years after they had already paid me. Some did, some didn't, but I was still liable. On top of that I had a fine to pay, which was over £10,000. My stomach dropped when I realised I had to pay this. I sent a handwritten letter to HMRC (the taxman), explaining that I had made a genuine mistake and – amazingly – was able to negotiate great terms with them. I believe that the fact I wrote them a letter changed the way they treated me – there are human beings at the other end.

That's why knowing what's happening with your money is so essential. If you know this isn't your strength, find an accountant, through word of mouth or googling, who specialises in your area to do it for you. It does cost money, but I see it as part of doing business. If your business is just you to start with, then you might not need to register as a company, but let HMRC know that you are now a sole trader. Later, an accountant can help you decide whether you want to become a limited company (which if you're in the UK means you have to register with Companies House).

You can find out the details of both options at gov.uk/set-up-business.

<u>4   PROTECT YOUR BRAND</u>

If you create a name for your brand, you have to get a registered trademark to stop other people using it for their own purposes. It was a long while before I trademarked some of my ventures. You can use what's called a 'trademark attorney' to help you, or you can use the Government's 'Right Start' service if you want to check your application meets the rules for registration (at the time of writing, the service starts at £100).

<u>5   LISTEN TO OTHER PEOPLE</u>

Another mistake I see people make is not seeking out the help of others who know how businesses are run. Early on, I was looking for investors in a business idea I had, and asked my former boss at Base79 if we could have a chat. I was all excited – and then he started asking questions that showed the holes in my plan: 'So, why would you do this?', 'How does that work?', 'What happens when … ?' *Gosh … I hadn't thought of that.* In that moment, I felt broken. I abandoned that particular idea – and it was the right thing to do. Success doesn't mean blindly holding onto something that's not going to work.

Boss lessons

As an employer, I faced a real learning curve. You can't just give people an envelope of cash! If you want to set up a legitimate business, you need to treat your employees with care, from providing HR services, to being on top of contractual agreements and payment terms, sorting out pensions ... the works! I've used freelancers and now use a combination of full-time salaried team members and additional hands on deck when I need them. I used to simply pay people via PayPal, but as my business grew I knew I needed to make it more official, especially for the team members who were truly contributing to the growth of my business. As a boss it's important to meet all legal requirements, and I had to get someone in to walk me through the steps I needed to be a fully fledged employer, following laws about internships, PAYE, minimum wage thresholds and even things like pension contributions. I remember thinking: *What's that?* I didn't even have a pension myself when I learned that I had to set them up for the people who work for me. I've since outsourced a lot of my HR duties and I work with a company who manage PAYE and pensions for my team, so at least I know it's all sorted. Eventually, when I am big enough, maybe I'll handle it all in-house. Who knows?

But the biggest lesson of all, for me as a boss, had nothing to do with rules or regulations: it was realising that when you employ people, it's not all about you anymore - you have to put them first ...

When you're the problem

There was a moment when I actually had seven people working for me. I didn't know *why* I had seven people working for me, not exactly. But I'd made a little bit of extra money and wanted to invest in growth. The idea was to improve my website and increase affiliate traffic (the number of people visiting other websites that I'd recommended on my website) so that I could make a bit of extra money from the sale of any products bought as a result of my website recommendations. At the same time, I wanted help with my hair extensions company: managing the social media, managing our suppliers and dealing with the logistics company I had hired. There was so much paperwork, documentation and numbers to take care of. So, I arranged to have all these people in place – and just assumed that they would know what to do.

Of course, business doesn't work like that, as I soon found out. The truth was, I took on too many people, and I didn't know how to lead the people I had in my office full time. Managing people is really hard, especially if you're still creating, as I was, and aren't able to dedicate yourself to this. So, they were all there, physically. But I wasn't: I was up and down, in and out of the country, I just wasn't present. It was almost like a unicorn came into the office when I appeared – it was that rare!

Unsurprisingly, the situation crumbled in about three to four months. I had to say, 'I'm really sorry. This isn't working', and let most of them go. It was very difficult, and the most painful thing, in one way, was that I realised I had been the problem. I wasn't there on a regular basis; I wasn't consistently giving people updates. I assumed that everybody thought the way I did: that they would just know how I wanted things done.

Managing myself

I had to take a moment to reflect on what it takes to be a good leader. I realised that I needed to make sure that I was there consistently: giving feedback, tracking performance, and making people feel like they were worthwhile. Now I have far fewer people working for me, but they all feel welcome.

Then, learning from experience, I made sure I had each person focusing on one area only. Previously, I would have them all looking after multiple different aspects of the business: they were kind of helping me; they were kind of helping the hair extensions company; they were kind of writing for the website. Now my team have clear roles. For example, I've someone who is on my product businesses, and she has the autonomy to hire people to support her if she wants to. I have someone who solely looks after me, my deals, what I'm up to. She is on that, all day, every day. And neither of them knows what's going on everywhere else in my business, whereas previously everybody knew about everything.

Keeping focus

That experience also taught me to focus my energy on the projects that are important to me. For instance, as I mentioned, I had started out wanting to create loads of affiliate traffic. But when I was honest with myself, I realised I didn't really care about that: my heart wasn't in it. And if you're just doing something solely to make money, it's never going to work. So I cut that area of my business and concentrated on what I really cared about. Once I'd done that, I was much clearer on my business needs: I needed assistance in editing video, because I create so much content. I couldn't call on my friends or my husband to help me take photos any more. I needed someone to help me out! And I needed someone to help support and manage what I was doing day-to-day. Since that time, I have had to do that on more than one occasion – cut the stuff that doesn't matter to me. The reality is, even if a venture is successful that doesn't mean it's the path you should take.

For instance, back in 2015, I launched a company called Collate

London. My aims were 1) to stage an event that would bring brands and influencers together in a physical space and 2) to generate a beauty box that we'd supply at the event, which would later be offered as a monthly subscription to customers. My idea was to curate a lifestyle box that was UK-focused: beauty products, notepads, pens, makeup wipes and so on. Y-HAIR was already up and running, so we were going to use the same fulfilment company to send out the orders. We had arranged partners to supply the products, working with established and up-and-coming brands. And our first event that year was a big success.

However, I soon realised that the challenge would be the scalability of our model: how could we grow this business? In this case, we had relied on partner brands supplying sample-sized products for the boxes. I realised that while a brand may give you 100 free samples, that same brand may not be in a position to do so every month – or to give you 5,000 as your business starts to grow. We would have to continually find new partners or pay for them. When I did a profit and cost analysis – simply, working out how much it would cost to finance this project, and the returns I could expect – I realised it didn't look so good: the box would become too expensive to appeal to our market.

That's how I made the decision that I didn't want to progress that business. My personal life also played a part – I got pregnant shortly after that and realised I couldn't do it all. I want to mention that, because business is not just about the numbers. Your own situation will always play into what's going on – and that's OK. So I didn't follow that project through. I had 100 excuses at the time, but in the end I admitted to myself, *No, I don't want to do this*. These days, I am careful of spreading myself too thin.

Why I love to fail fast

Having to let people go was a setback for me – and not the only one I've faced! But I'm not scared of failing. You just have to fail quickly. Try something, see how it goes. If it fails, do something else. Learn from it – in every failure there's a lesson – but a lot of people dwell on their failure, and then don't try again because they're scared of failing again. I almost like failing! It spurs me on. I tell myself, *Next time, this is how I'm going to do it. This is how I'm going to be. This is what I'm going to do.* If you want to be successful, failure – and overcoming your failures – is just part of that journey.

Every day I'm hustlin' (because it never stops)

By a lot of people's definition – and my own – I am successful these days. I'm doing something I love, and making a good living. And yet I never get caught up in my success, because I almost feel like it could disappear in a second. I don't have those *Woo-hoo, I made it!* moments. My attitude is, *OK, what's happening next?*

It's how I'm wired: I set myself one goal then, once I've hit that, I need more goals. It motivates me. However, I'm working on celebrating each success as it happens: it's great to be looking forward to the next achievement, but you've got to enjoy the moment.

10 | A woman's world

As a woman in business, there are certain things I've noticed – and learned – which I want to share with you. First, I do see differences between how men and women operate in a work environment and, of course, on a broader level too. I don't think we women always prioritise money as much as men do – and I am not going to tell you to start doing that! But I do think we can all do with chucking away the expectation that someone else is going to provide for us.

What I really feel about (some) men

I'm not traditional: I would definitely always offer to split the bill on a date. Don't get me wrong, if he pays that's really nice – but I've met plenty of guys who make a point of splashing the cash and making sure you know how much money they have, and they're all douchebags! Men with money, if anything, ring my alarm bells if they show-off about what they have.

What I *do* think is important when you go into a relationship is that you share similar attitudes to work and money. My husband, Mike, is a lot like me in this respect: he was always an earner. Growing up, he had a newspaper route. At university, he didn't even take out a student loan: he paid his fees himself, working as doorman at nights and coaching football to young adults, and he lived at his parents' house to save money. He was the same as me: frugal, putting money aside. When we met, he used to shop in charity shops and he had the crappiest car: a clapped-out Peugeot that you could hear before you could see it! When it rained the rain would drip in. The windows didn't work, so you'd have to use your hands to pull them up or down. When we would go out to the clubs, we used to park round the corner so no one could see what we were driving. He didn't care, but I was keeping up appearances! Until, eventually, I decided I didn't care either. *Whatever.* I was just happy to have somebody who looked after me so well, always happy to pick me up or drop me off places. Who cared about the car?

Just because he wasn't throwing notes around that didn't mean he was tight in any way. We would always treat each other: I would buy him stuff from H&M that I'd spotted, and he would do food shops for me when I was broke – there was no issue around money, because we were both generous with it towards each other. But we would treat each other within our means. And what all that meant was that Mike was able to buy his first house when he was twenty-three, and begin renting it out as a landlord, before he even had what some might see as his 'proper' job post university. That just shows how much all your part-time work – side hustles – can add up.

Don't wait for someone else to get rich

We all know that if you are in a couple, it can help you financially – you split the rent, the bills, and the rest of it. Mike and I were able to get on the property ladder together, which was definitely easier than doing it on my own. That said, if I'd have stayed single I would still have worked just as hard to buy my own place; it would just have taken me a bit longer. I definitely don't want you to wait for anybody else to allow you to be financially stable: the reality is, people can come into your life, and then leave it, so you want to be established in your own right.

There are no shortcuts here: again, it's just about my philosophy of working a little harder, trying to find extra work or opportunities, and putting money aside where you can. If you're single, your time is your own, so it really is a great opportunity to be selfish: to work really hard on your own goals and dreams. Use your weekends and evenings to build your mini empire or establish your hustle on the side – because when a relationship comes along, you'll just want to use that time to cuddle on the sofa.

Finding our voices

As a woman, your voice has to be heard. Working in the City – which is a very male-dominated environment – I noticed that even people that had nothing to say would speak up. One study found that in mixed meetings men will speak for 75 per cent of the time! Which, to be honest, does not surprise me. In meetings, I noticed some of my male colleagues would make sure that they asked at least one question – and it might be the most obvious, irrelevant question, which we all knew the answer to – just to be heard. Because they know that getting noticed in the workplace is important.

That didn't come naturally to me, and I still don't like the idea of talking just for the sake of it. But as I progressed in my career, inevitably I came to know my business very well. That gave me the confidence to speak up more in the meetings. If there was a problem, I'd say so: 'But this is wrong. That should be like that.' People respected that, because I had the knowledge and experience to back up the points I was making.

If you're not confident in speaking up straight away – and I know I wasn't at the start of my career – and worried about your message coming across messily, you can write a point down as it occurs to you, then say it. You can even do that in advance of a meeting, if you take a few moments to think.

. . . .

LIFE LESSON: Some people will tell themselves, 'I'll save my question till later' or, 'No, this isn't a good time.' Those are excuses. Just ask the question!

. . . .

You don't have to be 'girly'

Another thing I've noticed relates to how we handle our emotions in the workplace. In my industry, I have seen the pressure get to people – at times, I've got the sense that an influencer has emotionally disconnected and thought to herself, *I'm done with this.* But to stay the course, you've just got to keep going, staying strategic, as I've seen many guys in the industry doing behind the scenes. Recently, I was at an event with a male influencer, and I was struck by the way he behaved. He took control of the room that night, even telling me, 'No, Patricia, stand up front' – he was reminding me that I shouldn't be afraid to take my rightful place in that situation. He wasn't rude about it – I love him! – but I could really see why he's at the top of his game. While it's still important to value the softness and the emotional side that women have traditionally been praised for, I don't think any of us should be afraid to take control, shrug off the setbacks, and promote ourselves.

Which leads me on to another important point: don't be scared of not being the archetypal girl. For a long time, this was something I felt very self-conscious about, that I'm not the most girly girl or the most demure, ladylike woman. I'm quite loud and bossy. People can expect you to be a certain way. Particularly when I was starting out, I used to always get comments online of, 'She's so arrogant. She's so loud. Why is she so happy? Why is she so this … ?' I had moments where I was like, *Man, should I be a bit more mild-mannered?* I tried it for a while. I actually used to try to pull myself back, dial myself down a little, because I wanted to come across as a little bit more peppy – sweet and 'feminine'. On YouTube, I was much calmer. 'Hi, I'm Patricia. I like flowers in the morning.' I was trying to be like other women I saw online, softer and more demure.

Now, there's nothing at all wrong with women who are like that! But I'm not that kind of woman. It won't come as a surprise to you to learn that that strategy didn't stick for very long. There was a point where I thought, *You know what? I can't do this.*

Even if some people don't like it, I cannot keep this up. I need to be me. I relaxed, and shook off the shackles of pretending to be something I wasn't. I felt like I could breathe again. After that, I actually saw my growth and interaction improve, despite what the haters had been saying. Being myself helped me blow up!

• •

LIFE LESSON: It's so important for us all to be ourselves. We don't have to fit into a box of what is supposed to be 'womanly', just because we're women.

• •

Trust yourself

I've heard from other women in business who found that if they had a male business partner, he would often end up managing the numbers and the contracts and the business meetings, while she ended up looking after the creative aspect. But that means you're giving up a great deal of power and control. I know it can be tempting, if certain aspects of business don't come naturally, to not focus on them. Say, if you're a creative, visual type, I can see why you might much rather focus on designing your website than anticipating cash flows – how much money is coming in and out of your company – for the next year. But, if you're trying to make your business a success, you need to know what's happening with all the stuff that might seem less appealing: for example, you need to read every contract, and understand exactly what that dull-seeming language means you're agreeing to, before you sign on the dotted line.

I've found that sometimes women, even those of us who are self-employed or entrepreneurs, can be a little scared to embrace this side of things. I don't think that's all down to us – even now, some people think I don't know what I'm doing, until I open my mouth and I show them! Then, they see my media packs, where I set out my rates; they see my invoicing tools; they see my Excel spreadsheets; and they see that I'm confident that I know what I'm talking about. Because I do know my business, inside out.

So don't be scared: if I can do this, so can you. Go on to the government websites to find out what you need to know or, if that doesn't appeal, find an accountant, grab a cup of coffee and ask them: I am always talking to mine, and I've also got used to reading my balance sheets and my accounts, and I understand what the numbers mean. That's how you build that confidence in your abilities and knowledge – so you don't end up letting bossy men tell you what to do and how to do it!

• •

LIFE LESSON: The power is in the numbers. Don't give away control of your numbers.

• •

Remember: *You* are your business. You are your brand. You can do what you want to do.

11 | Discovering who you are (and what you value)

As much as I have worked hard, money and material success are not top of my list of priorities. There are people who are very rich, and successful, who still aren't satisfied. And there are people who have much less and they have higher levels of happiness. Studies show that there is a correlation between earning more and happiness, as you'd expect – I know first-hand the stress and worry that having no money can cause. But, at the same time, it's not quite that simple. A 2010 Princeton University study found that beyond a certain level of wealth people's happiness plateaus: once the people they surveyed were earning more than $75,000 (around £50,000) a year, more money had no effect on their everyday happiness.[1]

And we've all heard the tales of lottery winners whose instant riches caused chaos and sadness in their personal lives. The twenty-first-century version seems to be tech billionaires who find

---

1 https://www.theguardian.com/money/2016/jan/07/can-money-buy-happiness

themselves adrift when they sell their companies for eye-popping sums. Some even admit it! After Markus Persson, the programmer who came up with video game Minecraft, sold his company to Microsoft for $2.5billion in 2014, he made headlines by tweeting about how he really felt: 'Hanging out in Ibiza with a bunch of friends and partying with famous people, able to do whatever I want, and I've never felt more isolated.' OK, so later he apologised to the 'people out there with real problems'! But what do you do if you get everything you ever wanted? You can have all the money in the world, but lose yourself in the process.

That's why, in this chapter, I'm going to encourage you to look inward to define what really matters to you – and who you want to be, when all the crap's stripped away …

You've got to know yourself. Stay true to yourself. You've got to be honest about who you are. We've all heard that advice. But what that doesn't take into account is *your* agency in deciding what kind of person you are. You have the power to shape who you are: through the choices you make, the thoughts you focus on, the ideas you adopt. For example, I used to think that someone was either a morning or a night person. Then I realised that it was in my power to be both! I'm an all-day person because I have to be, because I've chosen to be a mum and have a busy job. The choices I've made throughout my life have formed who I am today and helped me uncover who I want to be.

Choosing who I wanted to be

Often, it's adversity that teaches us who we really are: when we're tested, that's when we make the choices that define us as people. I was fourteen when I made a choice that would change the whole trajectory of my life, although I didn't realise quite how significant it was at the time. I didn't enjoy those teenage years very much. I'd been at one secondary school for a year, then my sister, who was in the year below me, moved to a different school. Mum wanted us to be together, so I followed Maureen there. But I was put in all the lowest sets, because the teachers didn't really check to see what I was capable of academically. Through that, I ended up hanging around with all the kids who weren't doing so well in class, and were seen as 'bad'. They became my friendship group. Yet the truth was, I was relatively academic. Soon, I was finding the work so easy and was doing well in tests that I ended up being moved to the top sets for all my classes, and so was spending much less time with all my new friends.

Then the inevitable backlash started. My friends were asking me, 'What's going on? Why aren't you hanging around with us any more? Do you think you're too good for us?' So I started trying hard to fit in, to prove that I was still one of them. The upshot was, I was getting into lots of trouble and was even excluded from school on a number of occasions when I played up to the role of 'bad girl'. Still, the teachers always used to tell my parents, 'She's a good girl. She's really smart, but she's with the wrong group.' Eventually, I admitted that to myself.

Looking back, I was at a crossroads. I knew that there was a stereotype of how I could be, which was someone who was difficult and rebellious. I could have kept conforming to that and being what my friends wanted me to be. Or, I could be who I really was at heart: a girl who liked reading, who was quite academic – nerdy even! And I realised that I was OK with openly being a bit of a geek. I wanted to do well, and make my parents and teachers – and myself – proud, never mind what my friends thought. It was a turning point – a time of self-discovery.

As a result, I made an active choice to change. I didn't stop talking to my old friends, but I did stop feeling the pressure to spend so much time with them and conforming to their idea of how I should behave. I went so far as to decide that I was going to do whatever it took to become a better student – and one of my goals was becoming a 'prefect'. (Yes, like in *Harry Potter* but not as cool.) Our prefect system basically meant you were a clipboard-carrying hall monitor with additional responsibilities, which got you respect among teachers and a lunch pass. Yes, special! To be honest, I really wanted to show everyone I could do it, and that I was willing to put my rebellious stretch behind me. It was quite the turnaround. I was strong-willed, as my mum always said! I started going to the head of year's office every day and asking what I could do to help. 'Well,' he said, 'you can take all the registers to all the classrooms.' Soon, I was going by the office every morning to pick up all the registers and hand them out to every class, greeting all the teachers as I did: 'Hi, Miss.' 'Hello, Sir.' That suited me down to the ground because I loved talking to everyone. Because of my helping out around school, I became a fully fledged prefect. Finally, I was given a special prefect's diary and a special note to say I was allowed out of school grounds to have lunch. I loved it!

I was a year too late and technically not meant to be a prefect because of my track record, but I did it because I made the choice to change my path. It was a small step, but it showed me that if I wanted to be different I could, and it was up to me to make the choice.

More importantly, of course, I'd found my integrity. We all face moments in our lives where it's difficult to know how to proceed. That's when you've got to hold on to your integrity and do what feels intrinsically right for you. I've learned my lesson.

• •

LIFE LESSON: Everybody has the opportunity to create their own destiny. No, all the crap in your life won't just disappear overnight, but you can learn to deal with it better, in a more positive way.

• •

How I steered the course of my life

I really had to think about the direction I was going in, and whether I wanted to live my life according to what other people thought about me, or according to my own values. Of course, it's rare that it becomes so clear to us that we are at a crossroads in our lives. But the reality is that we are, all the time – every day we make choices and decisions over what we say, think and do that shape our path. And I really do think it's helpful to think about the direction you want to go in, too.

Growing up, my overall goals were to be happy and to be successful, and I knew there wasn't just one way to achieve those things. There were multiple different factors that would play a part in me achieving that aim. And there is beauty in not being too narrow about your definition of success: you open yourself up to the many different routes to a good life. But I did make choices that would, overall, work towards my vision of what I wanted. For example, I planned go to university, because I felt it gave me a better chance of being successful.

Of course, someone else might have a very different idea of what success looks like. Maybe someone wants to be a mechanic, so they start by working on cars at the age of fifteen and learning everything they can. Maybe they start a YouTube channel, too, when they share what they know with people looking to learn about car maintenance and save a bit of money doing easy-to-fix jobs themselves. Perhaps they get a bit of a profile through that and demonstrate their enthusiasm for the work, and it helps them save the money to set up their own garage one day. The ball's started rolling. The key thing is to think about what you want and take the actions that will help you be who you want to be.

In a similar vein, I knew that I wanted to settle down quite early because I knew my personality, that I could be a little bit, let's say, all over the place! I knew that being with one man would suit me. I didn't want to date around. I wanted to start a home. Getting married was something that allowed me to feel settled. *Right. I've got that sorted. Now I can get on with my life*! But not everyone feels like that. Some girls love dating, being wined and dined, talking to lots of different guys. I just knew that I didn't enjoy that. Maybe it's because I'm a worrier and I'd be fretting: *Is that guy really into me? Is he not into me? Is he talking to other girls?* I just couldn't be a dater. If I wasn't with Mike, I think I'd be single for ever, basically! I want one man who loves me, in a relationship that's secure and easy.

That's me. Something else entirely might feel right for you. Along the way I've learned a few important lessons, which I want to share …

1 UNDERSTAND WHO IT IS YOU ARE TRYING TO MAKE HAPPY

These days, I'm able to tune out other people's thoughts about what I should or shouldn't be doing. By all means canvass the opinions of people you trust to have your best interests at heart or who have relevant experience. But, ultimately, it is you who will have to make the call about the direction you're going in, over and over again. And, if you want to be in charge of your own life, there will likely be moments when you'll have to do what you believe to be right despite a few raised eyebrows. I'm lucky that the majority of people around me have been supportive of what I wanted to do, but there are always some who don't get it, especially since I'm in social media, a newer field.

For instance, when I quit my job at the Japanese bank, I just wasn't that fussed about what anybody else had to say, because in my own head I had planned meticulously for the future. Of course I told Mike, since we were building a life together. He was a little cautious. 'You're sure you want to quit your job? We've got a mortgage, you finally love your position?' But once he'd figured out that I was serious and had it all worked out, he said if I thought I could do it, I should go ahead and do it. That was it. I don't think I even told my parents! I just made the decision and went through with it. Mum understood. Her mentality has always been: *Whatever you do, just do it well.* She and my dad are proud of me no matter what I do. Naturally, my parents did like it when I went into the City. 'My daughter? She's in banking.' And when I left that safe, respectable job, it wasn't as easy for them to explain what I was attempting to do – a lot of people really didn't understand. But they do now (most of them)! If I'd listened to the odd auntie who had something to say about it, I'd never have gone on this amazing journey. Trust yourself and your trajectory.

• •

LIFE LESSON: When you are not true to yourself, you can end up lying to yourself: *This is fine, I'm OK with this, I don't mind.* It eats away at you. Just remember, when you say no to something that isn't right for you, it allows you to say yes to the things that are.

• •

2 FIND YOUR TRIBE

I've been very lucky in love – and by that I don't just mean finding Mike but in terms of the family I grew up in. Yes, there was discipline: my parents weren't stern exactly, but they were very protective and kept me and my sister really close. When it came to my mum we were like her handbags – always by her side! She was very loving, as was my dad: fun and smiley. I could run away from Mum and go to him if I was in any trouble. Then there was my sister, Maureen. We're so close in age (she's less than two years younger than me) that people used to think we were twins. Today, we're as close as can be. I'm not really someone who will make loads of new friends, because I call my sister four times a day and I talk to my mum several times a day. Maybe I'm a bit too comfortable!

But while I was lucky to have such positive experiences when it came to my key relationships, I realise not everybody has that. If you don't, there isn't a quick-fix to make up for that and I'm not going to pretend there is. But what you can do is work on forming healthy friendships. You can also make online friends, in the same way I did when I was feeling isolated as a student.

Being able to connect with people outside of your day-to-day world has so many more pros than cons, so long as you're careful about who you trust online. All of this applies if your friendships go bad, as mine did at school. Keep looking, stay hopeful, and remember that you will find your people eventually.

3   SPEND TIME WITH PEOPLE WHO SHARE YOUR VALUES
Once you're clear on who you are and what's important to you, it gets so much easier to recognise the people who enrich your life and share your values, and this applies to the people you work with, your friends and of course, your partner. When it comes to romance, I believe it's imperative to find somebody with who you're aligned in terms of your work (and play!) ethic, your spirituality, even how you might want to raise a child. In fact, a study of 5,000 people in long-term relationships found that after laughing together, sharing values and interests was top of the list for what they liked best about their relationships.[1]

Of course, when you first meet someone you don't consciously

1 www.dailymail.co.uk/femail/article-3425583/Why-DON-T-make-love-regularly-happy-marriage-s-series-transform-life-depth-study-really-makes-relationships-s-not-think.html#ixzz5Cuj5Toou

think about their values, but people will show their true colours over a period of time. You'll see the fundamental foundations of someone's character. Now, I've known my fair share of (excuse me!) f***boys, but not as many as some because I was undateable until I was seventeen! Loads of girls I knew had boyfriend troubles at fourteen, fifteen, and I'd be there thinking, *Well, nobody likes me.* Now, I see it as a blessing because I could get good grades and stay out of trouble. That's my attitude towards being single at whatever age you are: use that time to plan and build your empire. Someone great may well come into your life very soon, and you want to be able to recognise how great they are, and welcome them in when you're your best self.

I was lucky in that I met my husband Mike when I was nineteen and he was twenty. For me, it was very important that we had shared values. And over time I realised that he was exactly the man I wanted to be with. He's a hard worker, he's strong, but he's kind and humble. Those are the traits that are important to me. Above all, we just get on and we love each other. We're not the same person: he's very adventurous – likes camping and climbing – which I'm just not into! But that's not a difference that'll break us up. Likewise, we both agree on the fundamentals for raising our little girl. We are Christians, so bringing her up in our faith is really important to us. And there definitely will be curfews! She'll not be going out all the time. We grew up quite differently ourselves; I was a homebody and quite sheltered in that way, whereas he was out on his bike all day. He wants Grace to do karate; I'd like her to do ballet. I guess she can do both! But when it comes to the big things, our values align and that makes life a lot easier.

LIFE LESSON: If you get with a person who has a very different attitude towards money that could be a point of contention in the long run. If someone's a spender, and you're a saver, that's a recipe for disaster in my opinion. Because it's never just about the money: it's about responsibility, and your attitude to the future, and so much more. If you can, get with someone who's got a similar mentality towards money as yourself.

HOW MOTHERHOOD SHAPED MY VALUES

It's not just the choices you make, but your life experiences that will shape who you are and your values, in a way that can be really wonderful – and surprising! Motherhood has changed me in ways that I never expected. There was definitely a settling-in period that I was just not prepared for after I had Grace. I only realised later that, in the period immediately following her birth, I was not who I normally am. Maybe it was partly due to the hormones. There were times when I did feel like I was experiencing postnatal depression, as many new mums do. It took about five months for me to actually feel like me again. But the truth is, I *had* changed. I learned that once you become a parent your life is no longer about you. There was – is – a new sense of urgency to everything you do, because it's not just your life you're affecting – you're now responsible for someone else's life too. I learned to love in a completely different way.

And what I value in my life has changed. Some things I was bothered about before, I couldn't care less about now: being popular, being liked by everybody. Now, my attitude is more, *Whatever. My baby likes me!* So I am OK if not everyone else does. I also used to be way more concerned about being on the scene, being on trend. These days, I'm busy watching *Mr Tumble* or *In The Night Garden*. And that's OK! I have found so much joy in walks in the park, going to soft play, doing things that I would have found boring before – simply because I'm with my daughter. I can't wait to have more of those moments. And on the flipside, I now appreciate things that I never would have appreciated before I was a wife and a mother: quiet time when I have the house to myself means so much more, because I don't get a lot of it. No wonder it took me a few months to get my head around all that!

---

4 FIND YOUR WHYS (AND YES, YOU NEED MORE THAN ONE!)

So what matters to me today? What gets me up in the morning? Being around the ones I love is what makes me the happiest. After that, it's about what I'm able to create, my work. I love being able to come up with an idea and deliver it. I'm not looking for all my joy to come from work and I don't get all my fulfilment from my personal relationships. This is crucial. It's so important that you get your happiness from lots of different areas of your life, not just one. The experts back me up on that. Mental health, according to Freud, the founder of psychoanalysis, is attained when someone has the ability both to love and to work.[1] (I should mention that Freud also had some pretty crazy theories, but this is one of his better ones!) Some people call it being 'dual-centric' – having twin focuses at the centre your life. Ellen Galinsky, co-founder of the Families and Work Institute in the US, an organisation that researches these ideas, puts it this way: 'Everyone needs to have more than one thing in their life. We find people who are dual-centric to be most satisfied. If people put an equivalent stress on their life outside of their job they get further ahead and are more satisfied at their job.'[2] For me, work and love are the foundation of what I'm about: they are my purpose.

I'm certainly not trying to be prescriptive as to what your motivators – your 'whys' – are, but do give some thought to what's important to you, or other people will define your 'whys' for you. Because when you've identified your core values, they become your mission statement and you can use them to sort what matters from what doesn't.

· ·

LIFE LESSON: When you know your 'whys', EVERYTHING becomes easier.

· ·

---

1   https://www.freud.org.uk/about/faq/
2   https://www.thecut.com/2017/09/what-happens-to-ambition-in-your-30s.html

How to plan your own path

Take a few minutes to think about the life you want. What might that look like now? And in five years' time? And in ten? Where might you be living? How are you feeling when you get out of bed in the morning? What kind of office – or not – are you heading into? Picture it.

Thinking about what you want your life to look like is just another form of goal setting. It gives you direction. Along the way to reaching the life you want, you'll have some experiences that you haven't planned for, and a whole host of factors will impact where you ultimately end up. That doesn't matter. What matters is that you're on your way.

Next, take a moment to think about your values, what you really hold dear. Does the life you've planned for yourself align with those values? Do your goals and ambitions mesh with your personal beliefs?

If not, take a second to think about how you could build a life for yourself where you're working in sync with your values, rather than pulling against them. How would it look if, day-to-day, you were aiming for goals that mesh with your values? Because when you hit that sweet spot, the sky's the limit …

The beliefs I live by today

That's why I've thought about my values, and devoted time to thinking about who I am and who I want to be. It's not complicated, but it's really important to me that I stay true to these values and express them through both my professional and personal life. As a starting point, I've outlined these core values. They don't have to become yours, although every one of them could work for you, too, and I've suggested how.

1   I BELIEVE IN FINDING A PLACE OF PEACE

I'm a spiritual person. I believe in God, a higher power. I am a church girl at heart, although I haven't always been. I grew up in a churchgoing family and always used to go while I was at university, but when I came back to London and was working I got caught up in everything else in my life, so my spirituality became less of a priority. Life happened, as it does to all of us – there were moments that were rough and extremely difficult to deal with. I found myself regularly on an emotional rollercoaster, as my career and life became more challenging, and I knew I was missing something that had given me so much peace and joy in my past. I realised that God and spirituality were a fundamental foundation for me, so I took the time to reinvest in that part of my life. It was nice to return to a place of serenity.

MAKE IT WORK FOR YOU

Some people might find peace through meditation, some might even find it in art, or music, or exercise. Whatever it is, you need to have a moment that gets you out of yourself – daily, if possible – and helps you to cope with and transcend the daily stresses we all face.

2   I BELIEVE I AM THE AUTHOR OF MY OWN LIFE ...

... just as *you* are the author of yours. What that means is that there is always room for self-development, because you are in the driving seat, with the ability to decide your own path. Focus on developing yourself, so you can make a greater contribution to the world. It's so powerful when you see tangible improvements in your life, your outlook and your results, that you and you alone have initiated.

For instance, I have a tendency to be quite scatterbrained and waffly in my videos. I've had to reflect on that and focus on being a bit more structured in what I put out into the world. I'm still me, just more streamlined, punchier and on-message. I don't put everything I say or do in real life on the Internet. No one needs to see all of that!

MAKE IT WORK FOR YOU

Challenge yourself to try different approaches, so that you can aim to be the best version of yourself you can be. If something works, that's great. If it doesn't, then never mind – it's not something to beat yourself up about. Onwards and upwards.

3   I BELIEVE IN (IN A THING CALLED) LOVE!

To be able to give, receive and be around love, that is the most important thing in my life, and it's become more important to me as I've grown older. What that means day-to-day is looking after my family and contributing – be that by time, money or good vibes – to others. Giving something back can take many forms – it doesn't have to be as literal as giving to charity. Giving some good vibes, through a smile or some cheering words, to someone who's having a bad day can be just as impactful. That's one of the reasons I love doing my videos. Once you start approaching life in this way, the opportunities to spread a bit of love are limitless.

MAKE IT WORK FOR YOU

Look for what you're able to give to the world, not what you're able to take from it.

So be active in your pursuit of the things that bring genuine fulfilment. It's not all about money or number of followers. And anyway, those things will grow organically when you surround yourself with people who nourish you, and you live a life that's true to yourself and your values.

12 | Staying the course in style

By this point, you should be feeling more focused and excited about your future. I hope you've even set some goals. But how do you make sure you stay on track and not get knocked off course by all the stresses, problems and unexpected hurdles that you'll inevitably face? Here, I'm going to show all my tips and tricks for staying motivated, making good decisions and keeping hold of your integrity in the process.

How to quit dithering

It's true that when you've given thought to the life you want and what you want to do with it, it's going to be easier to make that a reality. But that doesn't mean you can avoid the hundreds and thousands of decisions that you're going to have make along the way to achieving your goals.

When it comes to decision-making, my approach is *Fail to plan, plan to fail*. I do love a plan! However, don't fall into the trap where planning becomes procrastinating. I know a lot of people who can get caught up with all the planning … and the planning … and the planning, and they just do not execute. For some, the planning becomes an excuse not to get the ball rolling. We dither when it comes to decision-making, because we can be scared of making the wrong choice. It's called 'analysis paralysis'. That's why I make sure I deliver on whatever I plan. One technique I use is to invest in my decision and force myself to make a commitment. That could be financial, signing a professional contract, or making a promise that you can't break. Even something as simple as putting down £10 towards something. It could be £10 you put into a new savings account when you decide you want to save more, or £10 you put on your PAYG account for gym classes if you want to get fitter. After I had Grace, I hated working out, but I paid for three months' worth of personal training in advance: I had to go. *That's my money that's going down the drain if I don't.* Making that investment in your decision flicks a switch in your brain, because when you don't follow through the person it burns is *you*.

This is a great way, if you're indecisive, to force yourself to commit to something. And if you're feeling worried that you've made a decision and haven't kept your options open? Good! One study by a Harvard psychology professor called Daniel Gilbert found that people are actually happier with the decision they've made when they know they *can't* change it.[1] Although we tend to think we like decisions we don't have to stick with, the opposite seems to be true. Commit to a path forward – and don't look back.

---

1   Explained in www.nytimes.com/2003/09/07/magazine/the-futile-pursuit-of-happiness.html

* *

LIFE LESSON: Over time, making a plan and following through on it will get easier. You can build that decision-making 'muscle' so you ultimately make quicker choices and don't second-guess your every move.

* *

There are some days you just need to power through

Sometimes, I create a plan and I get really excited and have all the energy in the world to go hard at it. Sometimes I coast: I'll keep going but it's an effort to not procrastinate on the Internet. And other times I have moments where I just want to sit down and watch Netflix. I've definitely posted online admitting that I've just had a week where I felt like I didn't get anything done! Accept that there will be peaks and troughs in your motivation. It doesn't mean you're failing if you're not bounding out of bed ready to grind every morning. We're all human. You need time to recharge. I believe in weekends!

At the same time, I've learned to be less emotional about my business. Sometimes my feelings get in the way of my work: *I'm not feeling like it today.* But, the truth is, you don't need to wait to feel a certain way before you crack on with what you've got ahead of you. If you do, you could be waiting a long time. Sometimes when I'm not feeling it, I beat myself up: *Patricia, get your act together*. Sometimes I let the Netflix happen! More often than not, I get my stuff done. At the end of the day, if you want to build your own future, you have to, although these days I try to have proper weekends, clear of work. I'm in a different position now to when I was starting out, when I had to work a lot in my free time to get to where I wanted to be. If you're honest with yourself, you know when you're at risk of burnout, or if you're just not getting your head in the game. Get ready to turn your plans into concrete actions, regardless of whether you're in the mood or not.

Not everyone will like you

You don't have to win everyone over to what you're doing. Some people will really feel what you're doing and what you're about, and some won't. That's OK. The very qualities that will draw some people to you will be the same ones that will repel others. For instance, I have always been quite chirpy and a bit high-energy – and strong-willed, as my mum says! So, I can imagine how some people could have found that grating at school. When I was about fifteen, a group of girls in the year above really didn't like me, not for anything I'd done but because of who I was. I might have been weedy-looking, but I always had self-confidence: I felt secure in myself, because I felt loved at home. I can imagine that jarred with them, particularly if they were trying to cover up the fact that they didn't feel so good about themselves. *Who's she to think she's all that?* I became a target. They'd walk into me deliberately, or push me in the corridor. I'd tell them to leave me alone, while privately telling myself, *This isn't going to last for ever.* But, at times, I wouldn't want to go to school because of them.

Particularly if I was on my own, my heart would sink. Some of them were quite aggressive, even prepared to get physical. I was bullied. I was scared. But I wasn't going to be a victim, as much as those girls wanted me to be. And, most importantly, I didn't change who I was.

While no one's trying to beat me up any more, confidence can still threaten people. So can success. The trick is to remember that if someone's got an issue with your swagger, that's on them. The truth is, in life some people won't like you – but some people will like you just the way you are. Focus on them, and don't give the rest a moment's thought.

• •

LIFE LESSON: By all means, I try to be the best person I can be. But I'm also true to who I am and what feels natural. You can't achieve your full potential if you're trying to hide your unique personality, or what really excites you, or what you love, to fit in.

• •

Putting the grit in integrity

Sometimes you'll make the wrong decision. Or, perhaps you'll do something that other people are not happy about, although you think it's the right thing to do. So, what *do* you do when you find yourself in a messy situation, particularly one of your own making?

Do you want to let it crush you, or are you going to learn from it?

I've had to learn how to deal with some daunting challenges as my following has grown. Take the time I was dragged – and I mean *dragged* – on Twitter. I was really, really upset. As emotions were running high in the run-up to the general election, I shared a few of my thoughts, including, *'I'm a big believer in self-reliance. I've never expected from the state and take responsibility for my own future.'* My intention had been to encourage those who were feeling worried about the outcome of the election and let them know that whatever happens, we roll with the punches and make our own future. But some people read that as: *Patricia doesn't care about those of us who are suffering.* They felt like their lives hung in the balance based on the outcome of that election. I hadn't meant to dismiss or diminish those feelings, but I'd been badly misinterpreted. The upshot was, I received an onslaught of angry tweets and messages that day. When it happens to you, it hurts. I could see this wave of people unfollowing my platforms and unsubscribing from my channel. Everyone seemed to be saying, 'Unsubscribe! Unsubscribe! We're leaving you. You're so self-reliant that clearly you don't need any of us.' My heart sank. *What have I done to my reputation? People hate me. What do I do?*

In the end, all I could do was keep rolling with it. I couldn't go and hide away. I had no choice but to dig deep and keep going. That didn't mean I ignored the situation: I addressed it on Snapchat. I was apologetic, because I felt I had been insensitive. I wanted to let people know that I completely understood why they felt so vulnerable during a very turbulent time. I made it right as much as I could. Then I moved on.

I carried on doing what I always do, creating content and connecting with people over my platforms. I told myself, *Patricia, let's make some more effort. Let's show that I care.* And, in fact, that month ended up being the biggest month for subscriber growth on my YouTube channel. It seemed to be a mix of people who had unsubscribed and then, seeing that I was making an effort to listen to them, had rethought their decision, and new followers who were attracted by the extra effort I was putting into my content that month. So, although at that time I was really scared and at a loss, I got through it. What's more, I used that situation to really push myself forwards.

It's OK to cry when you get knocked down. I cry all the time! Let out the emotion when something goes wrong. But then deal with it. If you're at fault and you've messed up, make it right as far as you can. Acknowledge to yourself that the reaction was awful, if it was, and then *move on.* Life is often hard. Everything that you face is an experience to learn from and it builds resilience. Some entrepreneurs intentionally put themselves in a difficult situation, such as one where they might lose some money, or something important to them is at stake, because they feel like it toughens them up. That's a bit much for me! But I get the principle.

When something crap's happened and I've survived it, afterwards I have a moment of *Wow. Look at that.* Every time you make it through a tough time, it builds your confidence so you can cope with what life throws at you next. Because as your life gets bigger and more exciting, the challenges you face can grow in scale, too. Rise to overcome them.

• •

LIFE LESSON: It's important to learn from every decision that you make — and that includes those that have an outcome you don't like. There's no point stewing in regret, but if you could have done something better or differently, or perhaps not at all, recognise that. Take what you can from the situation ... and move on.

• •

13 | The power of a pep talk

When I'm in a tricky situation, worrying about what to do, I give myself a talking to. I literally talk to myself: *Patricia, let's make more of an effort.*

Why is it so important to be your own biggest cheerleader? I'll tell you.

Words matter

When I was little, just a kid, I remember saying, 'I'm so stupid.' I can't even remember why, but I do remember my mum's reaction. 'Never, ever call yourself stupid,' she told me. 'You're not stupid!' It was something she was really firm about, that I didn't talk myself down. Although I was a bit difficult growing up, she never said I was 'naughty' or 'bad'. Instead, as I've mentioned, she called me a 'strong-willed' child. Because she knew how powerful the words we use are, and didn't want me to have a poor image of myself.

That lesson has stayed with me. That's why I often think of the proverb that life and death are in the power of the tongue: I take it to mean that language and the words we use are very powerful tools, and that we can all reap the benefits of positive self-talk. It's logical – we all know that we need to be careful with the way we speak to other people, because they could have a lasting impact. So why don't we take as much care in the words we use with ourselves?

It's really important to me that I send positive vibes to myself and other people. One of the things I love about social media is the opportunity we have to encourage and uplift others. Choosing my words wisely is the number-one way I make sure I spread good energy and not bad as I go about my business. And there's no better place to start than with yourself.

To deal with nerves, I talk to my sister. She's my rock. If you can find that pivotal person in your life whose opinion you trust and who will give you words of encouragement, hang on to them. It might be your mum, your dad, your best friend or your partner. There are also times in our life when we will need to look inward rather than to an outside source of support. You know it works when someone else gives you a boost, whether your boss says you did an amazing piece of work or your boyfriend says your body looks fine. So why not start to talk yourself up, too?

By using positive self-talk you can change your whole mindset, shape your moods and deal with the challenges and stresses of the self-made life. It might sound a bit intangible and airy-fairy to some, but they've not seen all the studies that support this approach! Here's how you do it …

Talk yourself round

When experts talk about self-talk, they are often referring to mental chatter, the unspoken thoughts that run through our minds. But I love talking. So it shouldn't come as any surprise that I will chat to myself out loud! And you should too. I really believe that the more you consciously and verbally acknowledge all your good traits and actions, the better your self-image. If you tell yourself every day, *You don't know what you're doing, you're lazy, you're ugly,* it begins to take its toll on how you're feeling, even limiting what you can achieve. Tons of studies have proven the relationship between the way we talk to ourselves and what we're capable of. In one, researchers had students throw darts after talking to themselves in a positive or negative way. The students who were asked to verbalise positive self-talk – even something as simple as the phrase 'I can do it' – performed a lot better than those who had been asked to talk themselves down.[1]

So why hobble yourself when you don't need to? Encourage yourself! Make an effort to use positive language when you are talking or thinking about yourself or your life – cheerful and kind, the way you would talk to someone you love. I myself am someone who can be very self-critical, because I am pushing for excellence, but I know that it's important to motivate rather than denigrate, even if you're a perfectionist. Now when I catch myself thinking, *Patricia, that was rubbish,* I pull myself up: *Stop.*

I pep talk myself. When I'm feeling a little shaky or unsure, I will tell myself, actually out loud, 'You're amazing, sweetheart', or 'You're doing well', or 'Don't worry'. Sometimes, I'll simply remind myself of my achievements. Everybody questions themselves when they get to a certain level or do something out of their comfort zone. *Do I deserve to be here? Am I even any good?*

---

1 https://www.ncbi.nlm.nih.gov/pubmed/1324109

When those negative thoughts start to creep in, stop. Just refuse to follow them any further. Then, think of something you've achieved, a factual reality that even you in your most fed-up mood can't argue with. Say, you're nervous about a test that you're studying for. Acknowledge what you've achieved in a similar situation: *You're smart. You're successful. You aced that last exam!* I do it all the time.

When I was working in my first job in the corporate world and questioning my abilities, I would catch myself wondering if I really deserved to be there, if I was up to the job. When I did, I would make sure to correct those doubting questions and counter them with some solid facts: *Patricia, you were chosen out of 4,000 people. That means something.* These days, if I put out a video that doesn't go down so well, I'll tell myself, *You know what, Patricia? That video might not have been your best, but your other video was amazing. Remember all the lovely things people said about it in the comments. On to the next thing …*

Say my name

Yes, I use my name when I'm pepping myself up. I know, I sound crazy! But what's crazier is that research shows that might actually help the positive messages sink in! Psychologist Ethan Cross at the University of Michigan led a study where people were asked to give a speech with just 5 minutes to prepare. As participants sweated away to come up with something, he asked them to talk to themselves. Some he told to refer to themselves as 'I', and the others to use 'you' or their own names. The study showed that the people using 'I' were harsher on themselves in their mental self-talk, telling themselves unhelpful things like, 'How am I going do this? I can't prepare a speech in 5 minutes without notes!' While the ones addressing themselves in the third person were more encouraging: 'Patricia, you can do this. You've given a ton of speeches before.'

Addressing ourselves by our names gives us some helpful distance. We always seem to be harder on ourselves than we would be on our friends, family or colleagues, and it puts us in the position of talking to ourselves as we might to someone else. So show yourself some love, and talk to yourself in the third person. (Just remember there are limits. Me announcing, 'Patricia would like a cup of tea, please' doesn't go down too well with Mike ...)

Surround yourself with positivity

It can be hard to get into the swing of positive talk at first. If the people around you are being negative, are you going to absorb that energy? No. You can find positive energy sources that offer a different message. They don't need to be people who are in your life already – online you've a whole world of optimism and light to explore. For instance, I'm a fan of Mel Robbins, author of *The 5 Second Rule*. What she does in the morning, lying in bed when her alarm goes off, is visualise herself as a rocket launching. She counts backwards: Five, four, three, two, one ... Then it's all systems go – get up and at the day! Mad as it sounds, she says that's how she was able to bring herself out of a really negative place, when she was unemployed and could barely get up in the mornings. One night she watched a rocket launch on TV and thought, *That's it. I'm going to move so fast that I don't think. I'm going to beat my brain.* (That's where the five-second rule came from: she realised that you have around a five-second window in which you can move from idea to action without your brain kicking in to stop you.) In other words, she was using self-talk to help push past the moment of indecision and get herself out of the state of inaction she was living in. And just making that little change – getting up on time – put her on the path to changing her mindset and shaking up her whole life.

I love her story. And when you're surrounding yourself with people whose energy clicks with you, positive influences, it changes the way you see the world. So, let yourself be inspired in every way by other people you think are killing it, who are ahead of you – they could be in the public eye, they could be your peers. It doesn't matter, so long as they're motivating you to be happier, more creative, more curious or better.

• •

LIFE LESSON: Invest in yourself, just as you would in your business. I am my biggest asset, just as you are yours. I am all about bettering myself and accumulating the knowledge to help me do that. I will pay for courses from inspirational speakers and business people that I admire – I've spend hundreds of pounds and not regretted a penny. I will pay for pamper days too! When I've been working hard, I'm happy to reward myself and relax.

• •

And you don't need to confine yourself just to the messages people you admire are putting out into the world. You can basically mimic and copy every step that someone else takes and put yourself on a similar path, achieving the same results or maybe even better them. It's like having a mentor ... even if they don't know it!

Personally, I get really inspired by Gary Vaynerchuk, the wine entrepreneur turned author and social media star. I love his work ethic, I love his values; he's a boss. (Sample quote from his book *Crush It!*: 'Love your family, work super hard, live your passion.' That's what I'm all about!) He is one of the people that I admire, whose energy, words and thoughts I can draw on for inspiration. It's like having my own little army of cheerleaders when I need one. Who can you recruit to make up yours?

Celebrate yourself

In a similar vein, it's important to celebrate your achievements when you've done well. Crack open the champagne for the big wins, if that's your style! I celebrate in my own way. Usually I'll put out a tweet, thanking my subscribers, because I couldn't really do any of this without them. Then the love begins! I'll enjoy my moment and be hunched over my phone scrolling and thanking people and liking everyone's comments. Sometimes I'll be in bed in the middle of the night, still peering into my screen. I've stayed up really late responding to people ... and then woken up bleary-eyed when Grace gets me up. But it was worth it, as I love all that affirmation and positivity.

However you want to do it, just take a moment and congratulate yourself. It's important to recognise your personal milestones, even the little ones. Why? Because life's all about enjoying the journey, as well as the end result. When you arrive at your goal, you'll only go and set a new one!

How to talk the (self-)talk

Now, I want you to write down what you think *you* need to be told. It could be anything at all. What's the opposite of that negative little voice in your head that kicks you when you're down. If you're feeling stuck, borrow my words! I always tell myself: 'You're beautifully and wonderfully made.' It ties into my faith: I am a creation, and I've been created perfectly. So, those words for me are very important, and remind me that I've been made for a purpose and that I will spend my day carrying out that purpose. But you choose any words you want: just remember, it's OK to say you're amazing!

Some examples, if you're struggling (and obviously it's important to replace my name with yours!):

> Patricia, you are good enough.

> Patricia, you are beautiful.

> Patricia, you are brave and strong.

It can be surprisingly hard to give yourself these positive messages at the beginning. You may feel a bit awkward, which suggests you feel some resistance to these ideas (and also underlines how much you need to hear them). So put some energy into it. Say your chosen phrase once or twice, whenever you need a little boost – but say it loudly and say it proud! Put some movement with it as well. Just as with words, studies show that what we do with our bodies can affect how we feel too. It's true: for a 2012 study, researchers at the University of Kansas asked people to force a smile then asked them to do some tricky multitasking. Those with a smile on their face showed fewer signs of stress than those who didn't smile, even though their smiles were 'fake'.[1] When I'm giving myself a bit of positive self-talk I'll bring a bit of physicality to it, too: I'll stand up, stretch, have a little dance. Do whatever works for you.

So, what do you want to hear today?

---

1 www.ncbi.nlm.nih.gov/pubmed/23012270

14 | Streamline the stress away

I'm a worrier. Partly because, growing up, there really *were* things to worry about: I was just a little kid concerned about her mum, who was working so hard, and whose dad had been taken away by strangers at the door. Who was going to knock next?

That tendency to worry has stayed with me, even though my circumstances have changed. If you're the same, I know how hard it is not to fret about what will or won't happen, or feel overwhelmed by your to-do list, or busy yourself worrying about what other people think. It can be crippling. When I was seventeen I even got a stomach ulcer from stress. It was really painful and I was in hospital for a week. I remember thinking: *What the hell? I'm seventeen years old with an ulcer!* Like I was some kind of super-stressed executive. The treatment was pain relief and antacid, which neutralised my stomach acids – and just time, because the ulcer had to subside otherwise I'd have been in serious trouble. I had a lot going on at the time, with studying and school, but I'm sure it was triggered by boy troubles. However, the bigger issue was me not dealing with pressure very well at the time.

Since then, I'll be honest, I'm still not the best at staying calm but I've developed better strategies for coping with stress, because life *is* stress. The truth is, the only time you're totally chilled and stress-free, with your to-do list all done and ticked off, is when you're six feet under! Here's what I've found works:

Don't let your goals become burdens

It's great to set goals, but not to beat yourself with the goalposts! Getting fixated on achieving a goal, whether that's a pay rise, a promotion, a project or something else you are desperate to accomplish, can become a burden. And, if you're choosing to be your own boss and build your empire, the pressure to get to where you feel you need to be can be intense. You might feel you're struggling financially while your peers are getting ahead in a more traditional workplace, climbing the corporate ladder and being promoted. Your future can look much more unformed and open-ended compared to other people's. That's incredibly exciting, but it's also why it can feel very scary when you step off the well-trodden path.

The best way to combat that anxiety is to enjoy every moment of your journey: to focus on the process rather than your progress. For instance, I've decided to create my own website for the clothing line that I've been working on. I could hire people to do all the support functions, but I want to do everything myself. I like the process. For me, this project isn't all about making money. It's about me being able to birth something that's in my head and put it out there by myself. I'm embracing every aspect, not fixating on how it might eventually be received. You've also got to remember you're doing what's right for you, and that you're on your own timeline and no one else's.

Resist the pressure to 'adult'

The same applies to your personal life. Before you start to compare your life with that of others, you need to identify whether the things other people have are even important to you. This is particularly important if you're going it alone as an entrepreneur or trying to do something else that's a bit out of the box, as it might seem that people on a more traditional route are hitting their goals – buying a house, say – earlier than you.

So, cut out the noise about what you supposedly *should* be doing. Ignore those '30 things you need to do before you're 30' lists. What do *you* want to do? Do you want the house and the picket fence and the kids, or do you want to be free to travel and experiment and invest in yourself right now? Do you only want a guy because you're under pressure to have a guy, or are there other things you might want to do? You can be single if you want to. You can date around if you want to. It all goes back to knowing yourself and keeping focused on what's really important to you.

Why not draw up your own list of what 'adulting' looks like to you? I'd recommend every woman go on a girls' trip, internationally if they can. After graduating, I travelled in Southeast Asia with a friend and it was truly amazing: it opened my eyes to the world. Or perhaps you want to find the book that's transformative for you: the one that you can always refer back to when you're feeling stuck. Mine's *Feel the Fear and Do It Anyway* – more on that later. Maybe this one will be yours! But you might come up with totally different things that you want to achieve in your personal life. I didn't learn to drive until I was twenty-seven, but you might put it right at the top of your list. The most important thing to remember is that everything might not be perfect right now, but it's a process, not a race.

Remember F.E.A.R.

... or, that fear is False Evidence Appearing Real. No one seems to know exactly who came up with that acronym, but whoever it was, they knew what they were talking about. What it means is that our fears are mostly in the mind – mistaken beliefs and projections into the future that aren't based on reality. These can limit you by stifling your ability to create, to seize the opportunities and take the steps that will better you.

How do you get past the fear? Feel the fear and do it anyway (so said Susan Jeffers, author of the bestselling *Feel the Fear and Do It Anyway* more than 30 years ago – it's still such a powerful message)! If you only do things that you're comfortable with, you'll never do anything new, and that'll hold you back. You need new challenges to build up an inner portfolio of situations you've handled and come out the other side of. Things won't always go smoothly. The first step will be a leap of faith. Sometimes it'll go right straight away. Sometimes it will go wrong ... again ... and again ... and again. It's those scenarios, including the failures, that build confidence. I do still worry of course, but I don't let that stop me. In time, as you make a habit of pushing yourself out of your comfort zone and achieving new things, your confidence will grow. Never let your worries stop you from doing anything. I repeat:

Never let your worries stop you from doing *anything.*

Worrying isn't a strategy

Whatever new stress I have, worrying won't make it better. But it can be hard to get out of that negative *it's-all-going-wrong* mindset. One of my strategies is to write it all down. I'm a pen and paper girl – I'll just splurge it all out, everything that's on my mind. Then (because I'm a planner) I like to come up with an action plan, with steps to tackle each thing that's worrying me. You can even skip the planning part, although I'd recommend it, because simply by jotting down your worries you'll clear your mind to focus on what's in front of you. A University of Chicago study showed that nervous students increase their marks by nearly a whole grade if they try writing about their fears just before sitting down to take a test.[1] You can turn to this technique whenever you're feeling low, overwhelmed or anxious. Just pick up that pen.

Healthy body, healthy mind

It's true: it's very hard to cope with all that's coming your way and kill it professionally or personally if you're not treating your body right. So I do make sensible choices. I take my multi-vitamins, I exercise, don't smoke. I eat relatively healthily (although I do love a takeout. Mmm … chicken wings). Sleep's imperative for me to feel good, so I try to get a solid six to seven hours every night. I don't drink coffee very much any more, since I noticed that I felt very groggy if I hadn't had a cup and I didn't want to have to rely on something to make me feel normal. So I detoxed over four days, not drinking a drop. I felt awful at the time, headachy

---

1 https://news.uchicago.edu/article/2011/01/13/writing-about-worries-eases-anxiety-and-improves-test-performance

and out of sorts, but now I feel better for it. These days, I'll have coffee as a treat. I'm the same with alcohol. I'll have a tipple here and there, because I like the taste of red wine or a really sweet cocktail. But I save it for when I'm out and about rather than drinking to relax at home. I never picked up that habit: I didn't get really drunk when I was a student because I was so broke. I'd still rather buy clothes!

And I'd recommend you don't rely on alcohol or any other substance to help you feel relaxed when life and work start getting crazy, as they will. Find an alternative crutch that's going to improve your life and not stick to your waistline or hammer your liver. When I'm upset, I know I eat a lot. So I give myself a little pep chat: *Patricia, go to the gym. You're going to feel relaxed and get your body in shape.* I've also switched out milk chocolate for dark chocolate, because I find it harder to eat so much of it. I'm not going to pretend I always manage to get down the gym. Similarly, I'd love to be an early riser. My goal is to wake up at 6 a.m. or earlier so I can fit in a workout, and maybe a walk in the park, then deal with all my emails. I wish! Realistically, I am up after seven, when my daughter starts getting active – she's my alarm clock. Here's the thing: I am not perfect. I want to be an early-morning person, but change takes time. I know by now that you have to relax into self-improvement, rather than use it as just another way to pile more pressure on yourself. (Anyway, I *live* for sleep.)

Do more by doing less

We're living in a world where feeling overwhelmed is the norm. We're bombarded with way too much, more than our bodies and brains have adapted to. Too much information, too many products,

too many ideas ... too many people, it can feel like at times!
Cutting through all that noise and streamlining your life is essential to really being as successful as you want to be. If I am thinking
and worrying about lots of different things, I become anxious.
What's more, it slows me down. So I've had to do some serious
streamlining for my emotional wellbeing. While I love a to-do
list, I've had to learn to prioritise what's really important and needs
to happen, while bearing in mind what I can realistically achieve
in any given time frame without losing my mind. And that means
taking some things off that list altogether, or planning to come
back to them later.

So, before you stick something on your to-do list, ask yourself
a few questions to check whether it really needs to be on there,
or if it's there not to serve you but to cater to someone or something else:

> Who wants me to do this?

> Who will it benefit?

> Do I need to do it?

> Do I want to do it?

> Do I have to do it the way somebody else thinks I should?

> What happens if I don't do it?

> Does it have to be done now?

If, after asking yourself those questions, you want to keep an item on your to-do list, fine. But don't be afraid of lightening your own load.

Focus on what really matters

When you've streamlined your life to cut out the people and obligations that don't matter, it becomes far clearer what does – and I've had to be even more clear about prioritising what matters since becoming a mother. It's not that I had any doubts about continuing to push ahead with my career. My own mum always worked and was brilliant as a mother too. But I found out it's harder than it looks. A lot of people ask me how I balance it all these days. The answer is, I don't really! The truth is, life's hectic, and running my business, managing a team, being a YouTuber, and being a wife and mother on top of all that can be difficult.

Straight after I had Grace, I started working again. I shot a video four days after I gave birth, then edited and uploaded it. I was on a shoot seven days into being a mum. And I was on the radio about two weeks after giving birth! I wasn't tired, I was just happy to be out and working. But, in time, I realised I was trying to do too much because I wanted to prove to myself that I could, even though I had a baby. Now I'm more relaxed about the fact that things *have* changed. Sometimes I'm late to meetings or skip events, because I'm too tired or Grace needs me. There are times that I don't finish the work I've planned because Grace and I are playing, or she's crying, so I find myself a bit late on deadlines. And there's always a sense of guilt: 1) that I should be working more, and 2) that I should be working less!

Scheduling has become even more important to me, because

without it life can get crazy. And now I ditch or delegate what I can't or don't want to do. If my daughter needs me – if she is sick, for example – I will drop everything I've arranged. As much as I make plans, they have to go out of the window because she's my priority now. Being someone who's so driven, the realisation that this had to be my attitude wasn't exactly difficult – there was no doubt in my mind that this was what I wanted to do – but it *was* a change to what I was used to.

There's a lot of mum guilt: everyone wants to have an opinion on how you should parent, but you have to parent in the way that feels best to you. I've been on the forums; I've read all the books. And there's nothing like actually parenting. Now, when I catch myself thinking, *I should be doing my work*, or, if I'm out or working, *I should be at home being a mum*, I give myself a break. I've realised that you don't have to do everything. You don't have to be a 'super mum'. You just have to get a bit of balance and routine, and do what you can when you can.

And, as I've said before, don't compare your life to others' apparent reality. Now when I see people posting family photos where they're all smiling and happy on a lovely day out, I know what kind of effort's involved! It might all look very simple and easy, but in reality, that little baby's probably only just stopped crying and someone's making extreme faces from behind the camera lens just to get her smiling. So I don't put myself under pressure to portray a certain image in terms of motherhood – it's not my thing. And people like the fact that it isn't perfect: I'll share that Grace is having a tantrum, showing them what mum life is really like, and they can connect with that. Similarly, I don't worry about setting an example. My goal is always to strive to be a better version of myself, but I'm not perfect. One day, my daughter will learn that herself! But I've a few years yet, thank goodness.

All I can do – all that any of us can ever do – is our best. So let's aim for that.

Beware the enemies of progress

I don't just streamline my to-do list. I mentioned before that I unfollowed a lot of people on social media who I realised weren't helping me to feel empowered. Give it a try! Go through your platforms. Are you seeing things that cause you anxiety or stress or frustration? Cull it all. You don't need that noise.

I've streamlined with people IRL too. These days, I surround myself with good people. That means I don't have many new friends but the people who *are* in my life are supportive of what I'm doing. Plus – and this is what's so great – they're also involved in their own amazing projects. One of my friends has her own clothing brand. One of my friends is a senior consultant. I'm just the one who happens to have a YouTube channel. Everyone is doing their own thing, forging their own success and we're happy for each other's achievements. I've also met people in my industry along the way who are collaborative, excited and open-hearted. So, my life is now full of people who are rooting for me and want me to flourish and I feel exactly the same about each and every one of them. But that hasn't always been the case …

I won't call them friends. Let's call them acquaintances. Sometimes acquaintances may look like friends, then you start to realise what's really going on: *No, you're not really my cup of tea. You know what? You don't make me feel good. And perhaps*

I can't make you feel good either ... because you're negative. For instance, at one point I heard that someone I considered a friend had been talking about me behind my back. This had been relayed to me by various different people who also called themselves friends. 'Have you heard what [mutual friend] is saying? Well. Let me tell you ...' I took a step back from everyone involved: not just the person who'd been talking me down, but also the people who were so eager to let me know about it. I thought, *Our mutual friend obviously feels comfortable enough to talk to you about me in that negative way, so I don't trust you either ... Bye!* I do not keep those people I call the 'enemies of progress' around me, and neither should you.

Letting go of the old lets in the new

The benefit of cutting those ties was that it actually made me appreciate my real friends even more. I realised I just should be spending more time with the amazing people I already had in my life. And if you're in a situation where you don't yet have those good people around you to step into the breach, letting go of negative people creates the space in your life for you to find friends that are more positive. Throw yourself more into what you're passionate about or what you enjoy doing, and you will find new friends through what you love. Don't let any issues you face with the negative people currently around you stop you from being you or doing what you love to do.

• •

LIFE LESSON: Surround yourself with people doing their own thing and doing it well. Aim to only keep around you those who have good vibes. It's all about those vibes!

• •

15 | Feeling good from the outside in

Let's shift a gear. I don't mind saying that as much as I've thought about my values, goals and how I want to shift my attitude through positive self-talk *(Go, Patricia!)*, I've spent time thinking about my exterior as well. I'm not going to lie! It can feel superficial to care about how we look, but we all know that when you're not happy with yourself on the outside, it's hard to feel good on the inside.

The social media space, in particular, can feel as if it's all about appearance. Now we've a world to compare ourselves with, rather than just the people we meet going about our day-to-day lives. I do value feeling the best I can be in every way, inside and out, and I'm going to share with you how I've got to that point. But first, I want to stress my number-one rule, because women in particular can be so hard on themselves in terms of their appearance. Which is …

Appreciate what you have

Experience has taught me this. I didn't always love my body. I wouldn't say I was extremely unhappy with my appearance, but I was always a skinny girl. I know a lot of girls, growing up, want to be slimmer, but I was very uncomfortable being extremely thin. I felt twiggy!. I used to wear jogging trousers under trousers to make myself look thicker, or two pairs of leggings just to look like I had a bit more meat on me. That was my little trick but there wasn't much I could do about the teeth or the feet. You see, I wasn't just skinny – I had buck teeth and long feet too. I came to the realisation that *I'm not the cutest*. Yet I didn't let the way I looked hold me back: I would try to disguise it, but it wasn't something that distracted me from doing what I wanted to do.

Today I feel lucky that I was an ugly duckling growing up because it meant that I was able to focus on other things: my humour, my smarts, who I was as a person. Once I was at university, I realised that there were people who would find me attractive and at the same time I felt better in myself. I was growing into myself, filling out a little more. In fact, in the years after that, I swung into the opposite direction: I went from wanting to fill out, to being chunkier, and needing to tone it up, especially after having a baby. That mum tum was real and I felt a little uncomfortable with it (more on all that in a moment). When I was a teenager I could eat McDonald's all the time without gaining weight. That's not happening today! It's important to embrace what you have. Your body is uniquely beautiful whatever stage of life you're at, but it will change. Embrace each part of it.

• •

LIFE LESSON: As I say, life and death's in the power of the tongue – and that applies to when you're standing in front of the mirror, picking your-self apart, too. Ditch that strategy! Focus on the positives and be kind to yourself. You wouldn't tell a friend she was fat and ugly, so why the hell would you do it to yourself?

• •

Releasing my inner 'bougie thot'

Feeling better about myself wasn't just about growing into myself. It was an inner shift, too. At around eighteen, I started to think, *You know what, I'm attractive in my own way.* That was the mentality I started to have. *I'm not going to be everyone's cup of tea, but I might be someone's whisky.* And a huge part of my feeling better about myself came from having fun with my style and experimenting with clothes.

Because I didn't have a lot of cash growing up, I didn't wear designer items or have the nicest trainers. When everybody had Nikes or Reeboks, I had Mercurys. Never heard of them? Neither had I! Sometimes I would be so, so embarrassed, because people would laugh at what I had on: 'Patricia, what trainers are you wearing?' I got so sick and tired of wearing those Mercurys, that I actually desecrated a pair. I cut them up, rubbed a bit of mud on them, and went looking for my mother: 'Mum, I need new trainers …' I'm embarrassed to say that it did work. I was able to get another pair, and I admit, I did feel a little bit better. Still, they weren't the worst of it: sometimes, I'd be running around in plimsolls because trainers weren't something I was able to have, given my family's situation at that time.

So, as I started to earn a bit of my own money here and there, with my part-time jobs, the one thing I loved to buy was clothes, and shoes. My look was what I like to call 'market chic': whatever I could find at Tooting Market in south London! That was where I'd dig out my bargains. I wore a uniform to school, but as soon as I could wear what I wanted, at the weekends or after school, I would switch out into my market clothes – my jeans, my cute little tops and, for some reason, a lot of crepe trousers. The material wasn't the best quality, but I wasn't that fussed about materials; it was whether I looked cute in it.

How I turned fashion rebel

For me, expressing my personal style felt like a huge release. I went to quite a strict church growing up, where the women were expected to dress conservatively, in long skirts and hats. Because Mum loved to dress me and my sister as twins in our matching flowery, girly dresses, I looked like a pensioner at the age of twelve! Now that I had a little freedom to experiment I wanted to explore everything, so my style changed a lot. Some days I'd be a rocker chick: I'd wear leather and a lot of black and chains – that lasted for about three weeks. I even cut my hair really short, shaving one side of it, and styled it in spikes with red tips. Unfortunately for me, that hairstyle stuck around a little longer than the clothes …

I didn't buy into the idea that because you're from a certain area you have to dress like this or wear what all the other girls wore! Often I didn't have the cash to wear what everybody wore, anyway. At one point, a lot of people were going around in Adidas tracksuits and trainers. No way! That trend was way out of my price range. I had to find something that suited my funds. That led to my being a bit more creative (and label-free). I'd go to the haberdashery and buy fabric to make little skirts, or dig out things from the market that were just a bit different to what everyone else had. For a while I went around in Indian slippers, covered in diamanté with curled-up, toes while everyone else was rocking their expensive trainers.

I do look back on some of my looks and think, *What the hell was I wearing?* But it was a reflection of where I was in my life and what I felt at that time: I was rebelling against what was expected of me, and rolling with that. Today, fashion represents such a huge part of what I do. Exploring my personal style really has shaped me as a person, and helped me discover who I am and who I want to be.

And it's still evolving! Now I'm at the point in my career when other people are styling me, which is a whole other adventure. For my *Glamour* magazine cover shoot, for the spring/summer 2018 edition of their new bi-annual 'beauty book', they wanted to change my look entirely and so gave me natural makeup. There I was, the cosmetics queen, thinking, *Why oh why?* I love a full face! But their team had a vision in mind: 'Take it all off, Patricia!' So there I was, in the natural look, with Afro hair, wearing really vibrant colours, which all felt very different to my normal glam. But I realised that sometimes you've got to be taken out of your comfort zone to make the next move forward.

And that cover? I got so much amazing feedback online: people were able to see me in just a completely different way. Experimentation is always worth it.

Set your own style: my rules

Fashion was always my way of expressing myself in different ways, depending on how I felt at the time, and to let me feel good about myself – that's why I still love it today. And I want you to be able to do the same. Here's how …

1 ENJOY EXPERIMENTING

To find your own style, my advice is to experiment – which means, have fun with it and don't take it too seriously. (Just picture me during my rocker phase, loving life!) I don't just take inspiration from designers on the catwalk. I love to look at what other people are wearing when I'm out and about. I love visual merchandising in stores: how they've styled their windows and mannequins. Above all, I enjoy it. Fashion can come across as a very serious business, where everyone's too cool for school and very poised, hiding behind their designer sunglasses. The truth is, it doesn't need to be that way. To me, finding your style is about having fun. Take someone like Rihanna, who's become a total fashion icon, darling! She is always changing it up and is never afraid to do so – some of her looks could get laughed off the red carpet if someone without so much swagger and confidence was wearing them. But she rocks it, whether she's in canary-yellow couture with a huge train at the Met Ball or wearing thigh-high giant Ugg boots to Coachella. Wear whatever makes you feel good, puts a spring in your step and helps you to have a better day. That's all it comes down to in the end.

2 STYLE ISN'T FIXED

When we talk about someone with great style, it can feel like you've got to find a look that suits you and stick with it for ever. When people talk about style icons, the idea seems to be that you've got to be like, say, old-time film star Audrey Hepburn in her famous little black dresses, and find a really identifiable, unchanging look. Fine, if that suits you, but that's not me (and I imagine even Audrey had her downtime days in jeans and kicks). Even today I wouldn't say that my style has settled. Bougie thot, I've called my current look: sexy but classy too. But that will no doubt change again. I've learned to accept that my style might morph on a daily basis, based on how I feel, what my body's doing or what I've been inspired by. That's OK. Some people might feel they have to define their style. No, you don't have to do anything, other than what makes you feel good.

3 TRENDS ARE OPTIONAL

There's a lot of pressure to keep up with fashion and all the new trends arriving almost every day. It's even more intense in the social media space. The most influential people are changing up their look in every shot. But I want you to take something important on board. They can do this because a) they've lots of money, and b) lots of freebies coming their way. That's just not realistic for most of us. I'm lucky enough to be in a position where I can indulge in my love of fashion, but I've still had to learn to step out of that trend-focused mindset and do what feels most natural to myself. I want my style to make me feel good, not just tick off the latest trend. Just because something's trending doesn't mean you've got to hop on it, too. In fact, it can turn me off a brand if

I see it splashed all over Instagram and people dressing head to toe in the T-shirt, the belt, the sunglasses, the shoes ... and on it goes. Yes, I've had Gucci fatigue! And as for underboob ... no, thank you.

4   BLAME THE OUTFIT, NOT YOUR BODY

There are clothes I will not wear, as beautiful as I think they are, because they do not work on my body. You've only got to watch one of my unboxing videos to know that: I'll try on a gorgeous jumpsuit that I love and find I've a boob popping out. Back in the packaging it goes! That's fine. Just because something doesn't look good on your body, doesn't mean your body is the problem! Don't even entertain that thought. Send that piece back and move on.

5   WEAR THE BIKINI

We can be our own worst critics, especially in terms of our appearance. Online it can seem as if everyone looks like a ripped Victoria's Secret model. I've felt that pressure, because I just don't look like that. In fact, not so long as go, I decided I wasn't going to wear two-pieces any more. No, those days were over. I'd be stuck in a grandma swimsuit on holiday. Then I caught myself. I thought, *Who bloody cares if I'm not completely perfect?* I rocked that two-piece, mum tum and all. The best way to face down a fear – and the fear here is that we're not good enough, we're lacking in some way – is to, as ever, feel that fear but do what scares you anyway. Which, in style terms, means ... wear what you like! You really will feel stronger and more at peace with yourself. Above all, remember the main question: what makes you feel good, outside and in? Wear *that*.

A bump in the road

But I won't pretend I was totally happy with myself, even when I'd found my style. When I was pregnant with Grace, I hated seeing my body change. I didn't like how I looked physically. I know now that there is a stage when you don't really look pregnant, but you do look different to how you're used to looking, and that was something I struggled with. When I had a proper bump – I'll be honest here – I thought, *Great, I really look pregnant now. There's an excuse to be fat!* But before that, when I was stuck in that awkward stage, I felt really unhappy with how I looked. Nobody really shares that with you, that you're going to feel awkward when you're pregnant. And in the very beginning when you don't look that pregnant, but you definitely look bigger and more bloated, you might feel really quite uncomfortable. You're not yet telling everybody that you're pregnant, but they'll kind of give you that look: *Something's up here.*

After I gave birth, I was catapulted into feeling upset again with what had happened to my body. I'd imagined I would snap back to my former self. I'd seen those women who have their babies and, ten days later, they're showing off their six-packs again. It can seem like that happens for so many women online. And that was just not my situation. I asked myself, *What's wrong with me? Why don't I have my six-pack abs?* I never had them before I had a baby, so I don't know why I thought I would afterwards! But still, I remember crying, thinking, *What's going on?*

It took me a few months to come to terms with things being a little looser, a little saggier. But nowadays, I'm way more comfortable in my new body. There are bits of it that I like, there are bits of it that I don't – much like the old one! I'm not averse to a little nip and tuck – I've had my fair share! – but don't plan for any more any time soon. But I've accepted where I am. More to the point, I am so thankful for what's brought me to this stage: having my beautiful daughter, Grace.

And that takes me on to …

My take on self-acceptance vs self-improvement

While I do like my body now, it's not a secret that I've also had cosmetic surgery. It's great to accept yourself as you are. But, equally, I believe that if you're experiencing all-consuming unhappiness with some aspect of yourself that you just can't accept, and you have the means and inclination to do something about it, you should go right ahead.

The first thing I did was get my boobs done – a breast enlargement. To be honest, I had reached the stage of obsession. I would think about them all the time. When I dressed up for an event I would just sigh and feel really unhappy. I was genuinely upset. Then, or at least in my eyes, a boob job felt quite taboo. I knew that surgery was an option, but I didn't think 'normal people' had boob jobs – not regular girls like me. However, I felt self-conscious all the time, and I realised the constant discomfort was affecting my wellbeing. That did it for me. *I'm not just going to sit here and be really unhappy about it. I'm going to do something about it.* I didn't even tell my mum, I just did it. It wouldn't be the first time I surprised her! Any regrets? Only that I didn't do it earlier.

That was what felt right for me. Some people can get quite upset when women make a decision to change themselves, but it's our choice. In the same way that someone else might choose to have tattoos, or piercings, or change the colour of her hair, changing this aspect of myself was something that allowed me to feel more comfortable with my body. And I was able to develop my bougie thot style! I like to be sexy and I have no problem with that.

Still, it was two years before I finally talked about my procedure online. While I was really happy with the results and I wouldn't hide that I'd had surgery or be embarrassed about it with anyone I met IRL, online is a different story. You have to be much more careful about sharing what you do or don't do, because you can face an intense response, both negative and positive. And, as a person with influence, I didn't want to give the impression that I was encouraging people to do the same as me.

When I did speak up about it, sure enough I got some backlash. I kept hearing that people were 'disappointed' in my decision. I understood why my announcement caused that reaction – and to those that did feel disappointed in me, I apologise. However, I'm all for self-improvement – and if that includes physically, then that's fine by me. In my eyes, having cosmetic surgery doesn't necessarily mean you don't love yourself. Maybe it means you love yourself enough to take a brave step and make the change you need in order to feel happy and focus on other, more worthwhile, things? You decide what's right for you. You do you!

• •

LIFE LESSON: Self-acceptance doesn't rule out change. And you have to make decisions for yourself, despite what other people might think or feel.

• •

Time to say goodbye …

Yep, that's it, you beautiful people! We've reached the end of our journey … for now. I hope you're feeling fired up, enthused and ready to kill it in whatever ways you've been busy planning. Along the way, feel free to come back to this book whenever you need a boost. Turn down the pages that you like, scribble your thoughts in the margins, underline the bits that strike a chord. Most of all, I hope that I've convinced you of one thing: that if I can do it, there is no reason that you can't, too. It won't be easy. But it *will* be worth it.

And I'm rooting for you …

My reading list

Ready for more inspiration? Here are some of the books that I've found helpful along my journey. If you don't fancy reading, just search online to find these writers and speakers giving interviews or inspirational talks.

> *Feel the Fear and Do It Anyway* by Susan Jeffers – this is the book I turn to when *I* need a boost. She explains that pushing through fear is less frightening than living with a feeling of help-lessness.

> *I Am the Problem* by Soozey Johnstone – a business book that won't send you to sleep! It focuses on leadership and the ways you can get out of your own way when you're trying to build your empire.

> *The Athena Doctrine* by John Gerzema and Michael D'Antonio – this is really good. It explains that it takes strength to be soft

and how women (and men who think like them!) will rule the future. It's about embracing the fact that feminine energy is very important – not something we always hear.

> *The 5 Second Rule: Transform your Life, Work, and Confidence with Everyday Courage* by Mel Robbins – this is the lady whose 'rocket launch' countdown to transform her mornings inspired me.

> *Rich Dad Poor Dad: What The Rich Teach Their Kids About Money – That The Poor And Middle Class Do Not!* by Robert Kiyosaki, with Sharon Lechter – this personal finance guide has been out quite a few years, but I found it helpful to challenge some of my thinking and beliefs around money.

> *Money Masters of Our Time* by John Train – another classic of its genre, this is all about how the financial big shots have actually made their fortunes and what strategies worked for them.